AN EPIC JOURNEY THROUGH THE HOLY BIBLE WITH JESUS

VOLUME 3
REVELATION AND ANGELS

KAREN MARIE PARKER

ISBN 978-1-63903-683-7 (paperback)
ISBN 978-1-68570-720-0 (hardcover)
ISBN 978-1-63903-684-4 (digital)

Christian Faith Publishing
832 Park Avenue
Meadville, PA 16335
www.christianfaithpublishing.com

Printed in the United States of America

To God, Jesus Christ, and the Holy Spirit. Thank you for the mystical experience when you and I were one in my kitchen on October 30, 2014. From that day forward, I have grounded myself with a devotional sincerity to focus on you being present in my life, to deepen my awareness of you in all things and how you sustain my life. I have faith that wherever you are taking me is where I am supposed to be.

I see your light and beauty in everything. I look to you for peace in the midst of death. I desire to know you fully as you are in me, and I hope that pleases you.

After you swept me off my feet and brought me into your wonderful light, I have this incredible need to thank you by doing whatever you need me to do for you and your world. I understand that I may get blindsided by some unexpected crisis, but I know that you are with me and that you will help me understand to the best of my ability. I humble myself not knowing the future or being able to grasp the passage through time, but I am certain my infinite destiny is sustained by you because you are the god of life.

In Jesus's name, I pray. Amen.

> "For my thoughts are not your thoughts, and your ways are not my ways," says Yahweh. "For as the heavens are higher than the earth, so are my ways higher than your ways, and my thoughts than your thoughts." (Isaiah 55:8–9, WEB).

CONTENTS

ACKNOWLEDGMENTS

On October 30, 2014, the Holy Spirit transformed my life to walk with Jesus. The mystical experience that I had was life-changing for me. Through sacred Scripture, I have learned that our journey with Jesus is epic. The Scriptures give us hope and a strong sense of purpose for surviving in this busy world. The era that we live in now is much more complex than it was for the patriarchs, but it is not complex to God. Sacred Scripture gives us an understanding of ourselves and of others and how to be thankful for the gift of life from God.

In the Old Testament, we encounter a God who loves and forgives us unconditionally. We learn about God's never-ending pursuit for justice and peace. He calls His faithful by name. In the New Testament, God came down from heaven and was born as a human being, Jesus Christ. With Jesus, the new covenant was the gift of the Holy Spirit who lives in each Christian. This Spirit is the breath of God, healing and transforming us to bear witness to the gospels in sacred Scriptures. Understanding the Book of Revelation and God's angels will take more effort to search through the Bible to find the references to these unusual writings.

In my first book, *An Epic Journey Through the Holy Bible with Jesus: Volume 1*, I took us through the sacred Scripture to get to know Jesus, why He came, what His Father expects from us, and how we can be the best person we can be in a fallen world. Volume 2 took us down history lane with the patriarchs, prophets, and kings in the Old Testament; Jesus's genealogy; parables; and miracles. This book, Volume 3, will include an in-depth look at the Book of Revelation and angels. There are many types of angels and their service to God. Each depict a certain attire and light auras that reflect their specific services. Plus, I have uncovered Scripture to ensure you with the truth about God's angels who give praise, honor, and glory to the one and only *El 'Elyon*.

I would like to thank the many great mentors, pastors, teachers, mystics, saints, scholars, theologians, writers, and musicians who have shared their knowledge of our Lord God, Jesus Christ our Savior, the Holy Spirit, and sacred Scriptures.

Sacred Scriptures are God-breathed, God-speaking, God's presence, and one way for God to communicate to us. With the help of the Holy Spirit, I hope to draw you to an understanding of these mysteries hidden in sacred Scriptures. I hope that Jesus will come alive for you and enlighten your own journey toward God and His heavenly Kingdom. In Jesus's name, I pray. Amen.

> Now faith is assurance of things hoped for, proof of things not seen. For by this, the elders obtained testimony. By faith, we understand that the universe has been framed by the word of God, so that what is seen has not been made out of things which are visible. (Hebrews 11:1–3 WEB)

INTRODUCTION

My Testimony

On October 30, 2014, I had a radical conversion with God who brought me out of the darkness and into the wonderful light of Christ. I wrote about my full testimony in *An Epic Journey*, volume 1 and 2. It was an incredible story for me to write about, but this time I want to tell you about the ongoing journey with Jesus. Even though that mystical moment was indescribable, I have learned that it was a simple beginning.

Spending daily life in contemplation for five years has brought me to the realization of God's presence, through Jesus Christ, is forever unfolding each moment of every day. God's presence is in all things and was before the origin of the universe. Every breath I take is a gift from God, and apart from Him, I am nothing. The gift God has given me is in my daily writings for Jesus. My son, Jake, said that I have become a prolific writer, producing much fruit.

> I am the vine. You are the branches. He who remains in me and I in him bears much fruit, for apart from me you can do nothing. (John 15:5 WEB)

Looking back to those few months after my conversion, I remembered an incident with my husband, Patrick. He came home one day from work, and I mentioned to him that I was going through my closets and getting rid of all my concert T-shirts (you know, the black ones with skulls on them). I was not going to be wearing them ever again.

He asked me to not throw them away in case I changed my mind again. He said that he did not want to buy all that stuff, an entire wardrobe, again. So I asked him why he thought that I would go back to that way of life. He just smiled at me and said that I have CD. I asked him, "What does CD mean?"

His reply was, "It is compulsive disorder. We have been married for thirty-four years, and whenever you get an idea to change, you get into a motorboat and head straight down the middle of a lake at full speed ahead, then eventually the boat runs out of gas. The ride's over, and you change your mind."

I laughed at him and said that, "Yes, I suppose I do. But if I have a compulsive disorder and you feel I may change, what would you like for me to change to?" I asked him if he would like for me to change this path that I am on now with Jesus.

His reply was a definite *no*! He said that he loved me right where I was and did not want me to ever change!

So my reply was this, "If my motorboat runs out of gas or breaks down and needs a mechanic, I will call on you, Patrick. You can put gas in my motorboat because I will never go back to living a life with Satan!" I did throw all those T-shirts, jackets, hoodies, and all my evil stronghold treasures away. I did have a little meltdown at the time, but nonetheless, they are gone forever.

Now I can truly say that my prolific writing, my fruit-bearing gift, has been my motorboat at full speed ahead! Jesus keeps my head above water, my husband keeps my motorboat full of gas, and God is good all the time.

> For it is God who works in you both to will and to work, for his good pleasure. (Philippians 2:13 WEB)

> All wisdom is from the Lord and remains with him forever. (The Wisdom of Ben Sira 1:1 NABRE)

> Now there are various kinds of gifts, but the same Spirit. There are various kinds of service, and the same Lord. There are various kinds of workings, but the same God, who works all things in all. But to each one is given the manifestation of the Spirit for the profit of all. For to one is given through the Spirit the word of wisdom, and to another the word of knowledge, according to the same Spirit; to another faith, by the same Spirit; and to another gifts of healings, by the same Spirit; and to another workings of miracles; and to another prophecy; and to another discerning of spirits; to another different kinds of languages; and to another the interpretation of languages. But the one and the same Spirit produces all of these, distributing to each one separately as he desires. (1 Corinthians 12:4–11 WEB)

> Inasmuch as many and great truths have been given to us through the Law, the prophets, and the authors who followed them, for which

the instruction and wisdom of Israel merit praise, it is the duty of those who read the scriptures not only to become knowledgeable themselves but also to use their love of learning in speech and in writing to help others less familiar. (The Wisdom of Ben Sira, Foreword NABRE)

Yahweh's Spirit will rest on him: the spirit of wisdom and understanding, the spirit of counsel and might, the spirit of knowledge and of the fear of Yahweh. His delight will be in the fear of Yahweh. He will not judge by the sight of his eyes, neither decide by the hearing of his ears; (Isaiah 11:2–3 WEB)

For we are his workmanship, created in Christ Jesus for good works, which God prepared before that we would walk in them. (Ephesians 2:10 WEB)

The world is passing away with its lusts, but he who does God's will remains forever. (1 John 2:17 WEB)

Let us do all things for the Lord and to His glory. May the peace of the Lord be with you always. Amen.

FOCUS ON YOUR FAITH

Today is March 27, 2020, and it is a time for all to focus on their faith during this time of the COVID-19 pandemic. Our entire world is affected by a devastating virus. Our great president Trump is taking steps to have an orderly system of precautionary measures in this crisis. Steps to take control of the crisis and not the panic. These precautionary steps that we are using now are protecting the lives of everyone possible, and we will be able to use these guidelines again in the likelihood of a similar future event—if we even live through this one.

Thousands of people and many organizations have come forward to help and offer their services as needed. It is in this unity that we see God at work. The coming together to serve each other is love, and that love comes from God. In a time of war, you can always find someone doing something good like feeding hungry children, or doctors and nurses helping the wounded and sick.

Faith, courage and peace are a better way to take control of yourself during a crisis than fear, anxiety, panic and chaos. In Greek, *anxiety* means "division" or "to pull apart," and in Hebrew, it means "to strangle or to choke." In these kinds of situations, Jesus tells us to not be fearful but faithful. Strong faith will bring forth peace, love, and unity.

Jesus came to teach us that this fear that surfaces in a crisis is really our own fear that we buried deep inside our souls to cover up a sin. A sin that we do not want to surface for the world to see. A sin that we need to address with God to walk through the gates of righteousness. When tribulation comes and we know that we have not reconciled our own sins, then fear, anxiety, and panic boil out because you are not ready. Well, maybe it is time to start now? Do some soul searching, and in your private time with Jesus, ask Him to help you through every one of those fears. Here are a few scriptures on what Jesus has to say about blindness versus twenty-twenty vision:

> Jesus then said, "I came into the world to bring everything into the clear light of day, making all the distinctions clear, so that those who have never seen will see, and those who have made a great pretense of seeing will be exposed as blind." Some Pharisees overheard him and said, "Does that mean you're calling us blind?" Jesus said, "If you were really blind, you would be blameless, but since you claim to see everything so well, you're accountable for every fault and failure." (John 9:39–41 MSG)

> Jesus said to them, "If you were blind, you would have no sin; but now you say, 'We see.' Therefore, your sin remains." (John 9:41 NKJV)

Jesus is talking about spiritual blindness. Ignorant men are not condemned for what they do not know. He came to help those who are ignorant, to understand Scripture and its true meaning. Most people in those days could not read. They relied on what the Pharisees preached and read to them. But after their baptism, they received the Holy Spirit and could understand their sins and confess them, then they would be pardoned by God.

"I was blind, now I see." (John 9:25 NKJV)

Now the Pharisees claimed to "see," to have twenty-twenty vision, because they were men that new the laws of Moses. They were confident in their wisdom, knowing all the sins that were forbidden in the eyes of God and believed they were pardoned by God. But their hearts were faulty, causing spiritual blindness, and Jesus knew that they did not practice what they preached. He knew that their self-inflicted blindness caused them to believe that God would forgive all their sins. But the truth remains that God knows the intentions of the heart, therefore the guilt of their sin remains unpardoned. This is where fear and anxiety come in.

> "The heart is hopelessly dark and deceit-
> ful, a puzzle that no one can figure out. But I,
> GOD, search the heart and examine the mind. I
> get to the heart of the human. I get to the root of
> things. I treat them as they really are, not as they
> pretend to be." (Jeremiah 17:9–10 MSG)

Pride and self-confidence are a source of condemnation. The Holy Spirit teaches us to come before God with humble hearts and confess our sins. With this reconciliation, God will forgive our sins, and this atonement will restore a broken relationship with God. Jesus will always cure our spiritual blindness and give us true twenty-twenty vision. In Jesus's name, I pray. Amen.

ANXIETY

By Douglas Gamache

"Do not be anxious about anything, but in every situation, by prayer and petition, with thanksgiving, present your requests to God. And the peace of God, which transcends all understanding, will guard your hearts and your minds in Christ Jesus."

—Philippians 4:6–7 NIV

I would like to talk about anxiety and try to explain what this passage means. Anxiety is a very serious illness for some people, and those who do have this illness do not understand it. In Hebrew, the word *anxiety* means "to choke," and when I learned this, it really put things into perspective. Anxiety is not fear; in fact, they are two separate things. A person with anxiety will choke their own life right out of themselves. Jesus does not want us to do that, so He tries very hard for us to understand. Here are a few examples of the difference between fear and anxiety by Max Lucado:

A fearful person sees a threat, while a person with anxiety imagines one. A person in fear of a threat results in a fight-or-flight response, while an anxious person creates a gloom-and-doom response. In unfavorable situations, a fearful person will scream to themselves, "Stop it, just stop thinking badly!," when worries start to settle in; while an anxious person will ponder and let worries settle in their minds and create all sorts of unnecessary problems that don't exist. A fearful person will have their pulse race when an airplane shakes in flight, while an anxious person will never fly because that plane may crash. Max Lucado has a great Bible study on this subject, and it's called *Anxious for Nothing*.

So what do we do about this nasty anxiety problem? Well, continue studying the Bible, and Christ will talk about it and how anxious people can come to rest.

> When I am afraid, I will put my trust in you. (Psalm 56:3 WEB)

> Therefore I tell you, don't be anxious for your life: what you will eat, or what you will drink; nor yet for your body, what you will wear. Isn't life more than food, and the body more than clothing? See the birds of the sky, that they don't sow, neither do they reap, nor gather into barns. Your heavenly Father feeds them. Aren't you of much more value than they?

> "Which of you by being anxious, can add one moment to his lifespan? Why are you anxious about clothing? Consider the lilies of the field, how they grow. They don't toil, neither do they spin, yet I tell you that even Solomon in all his glory was not dressed like one of these. But if God so clothes the grass of the field, which today exists and tomorrow is thrown into the oven, won't he much more clothe you, you of little faith?

> "Therefore, don't be anxious, saying, 'What will we eat?', 'What will we drink?' or, 'With what will we be clothed?' For the Gentiles seek after all these things; for your heavenly Father knows that you need all these things. But seek first God's Kingdom and his righteousness;

and all these things will be given to you as well. Therefore don't be anxious for tomorrow, for tomorrow will be anxious for itself. Each day's own evil is sufficient." (Matthew 6:25–34 WEB)

Therefore do not worry about tomorrow, for tomorrow will worry about itself. Each day has enough trouble of its own. (Matthew 6:34 NIV)

Wow, thank you, Jesus. You said that perfectly! Reading what Jesus has to say about anxiety sure puts things into perspective.

ENVISAGE

BY KAREN PARKER

Envisage is to foresee and contemplate a conceived idea of a desirable future event. Such as when God envisaged a remedy for man's restoration of the original sin, returning man to his former owner, God. Man had strayed so far away from spiritual love and immersed himself into material things that God had decided to devise a plan to recall man back to his soul and to an understanding of His gift of grace. The divine incarnation, or epitome of becoming embodied in the flesh and dwell with man, came through in Jesus Christ.

> And the Word became flesh and dwelt among us, and we beheld His glory, the glory as of the only begotten of the Father, full of grace and truth. (John 1:14 NKJV)

> Here is a trustworthy saying that deserves full acceptance: Christ Jesus came into the world to save sinners—of whom I am the worst. (1 Timothy 1:15 NIV)

Despite the sin that contaminated our human nature, God loves us and will always desire for us to have blissful happiness or to be beatific. First, Christ's crucifixion had to free us from this defilement before any repentance could be tolerated and accepted by God

Himself. Then a way of life must be achieved by virtue or a behavior showing high moral standards; the Beatitudes were established with Christ before His crucifixion. In sacred Scripture, it is called "The Sermon on the Mount."

Now when Jesus saw the crowds, he went up on a mountainside and sat down. His disciples came to him, and he began to teach them. He said: "Blessed are the poor in spirit, for theirs is the kingdom of heaven. Blessed are those who mourn, for they will be comforted. Blessed are the meek, for they will inherit the earth. Blessed are those who hunger and thirst for righteousness, for they will be filled. Blessed are the merciful, for they will be shown mercy. Blessed are the pure in heart, for they will see God. Blessed are the peacemakers, for they will be called children of God. Blessed are those who are persecuted because of righteousness, for theirs is the kingdom of heaven.

"Blessed are you when people insult you, persecute you and falsely say all kinds of evil against you because of me. Rejoice and be glad, because great is your reward in heaven, for in the same way they persecuted the prophets who were before you." (Matthew 5:1–12 NIV)

Follow after peace with all men, and the sanctification without which no man will see the Lord, looking carefully lest there be any man who falls short of the grace of God, lest any root of bitterness springing up trouble you, and many be defiled by it. (Hebrews 12:14–15 WEB)

For the love of Christ constrains us; because we judge thus, that one died for all, therefore all died. He died for all, that those who live should no longer live to themselves, but to him who for their sakes died and rose again. (2 Corinthians 5:14–15 WEB)

For the high and lofty One who inhabits eternity, whose name is Holy, says: "I dwell in the high and holy place, with him also who is of a contrite and humble spirit, to revive the spirit of the humble, and to revive the heart of the contrite." (Isaiah 57:15 WEB)

to proclaim the year of Yahweh's favor and the day of vengeance of our God, to comfort all who mourn. (Isaiah 61:2 WEB)

But the humble shall inherit the land, and shall delight themselves in the abundance of peace. (Psalm 37:11 WEB)

"Rejoice with Jerusalem, and be glad for her, all you who love her. Rejoice for joy with her, all you who mourn over her;" (Isaiah 66:10 WEB)

"For my hand has made all these things, and so all these things came to be," says Yahweh: "but I will look to this man, even to he who is poor and of a contrite spirit, and who trembles at my word." (Isaiah 66:2 WEB)

Through the Beatitudes, we can restore our spiritual love for God and cleanse our souls which in return will bring us back blissful happiness, peace of mind, rapture, or intense pleasure of joy and rhapsody and be enthusiastic about life again. Don't let demons destroy your envisage, your conceived idea of a desirable future with God.

He restores my soul. He guides me in the paths of righteousness for his name's sake. (Psalm 23:3 WEB)

TRAVAIL AND JOY COMETH

Travail is a painful or laborious effort that happens during the process of a transition of one condition to another and may also cause great emotional distress. There are three kinds of travail events that I would like to talk about: birthing pains, Jesus's crucifixion, and the end of times. All these events, Christ describes as birthing pains of a woman; but He also says that joy will follow, joy cometh.

> To the woman he said, "I will greatly multiply your pain in childbirth. You will bear children in pain. Your desire will be for your husband, and he will rule over you." (Genesis 3:16 WEB)

This was spoken after the original sin took place in the garden of Eden. Later, God provided a remedy for the original sin through divine wisdom, love, and justice. God decided to become man: He came as Christ Jesus. He wanted to cleanse, merit, and restore the contamination of sin that defiled human nature. He wanted to call us back to a spiritual life and offer us eternal life; this is our joy that cometh. Both events happened in the garden of Eden.

> Now in the place where he was crucified there was a garden. In the garden was a new tomb in which no man had ever yet been laid. Then because of the Jews' Preparation Day (for the tomb was near at hand) they laid Jesus there. (John 19:41–42 WEB)

Just before Jesus's crucifixion, his disciples were in emotional distress because they could not understand what He was talking about: pain and suffering, death and resurrection, and the Holy Spirit of Truth. Jesus's time had come to restore mankind with the Spirit of Truth and break the vindication, the original judgment of sin; this reality must dawn into the present millennium so that we may prepare the way for the coming kingdom, eternal life, and joy cometh. This is God's new covenant.

> Most certainly I tell you that you will weep and lament, but the world will rejoice. You will be sorrowful, but your sorrow will be turned into joy. A woman, when she gives birth, has sorrow because her time has come. But when she has delivered the child, she doesn't remember the anguish any more, for the joy that a human being is born into the world. Therefore you now have sorrow, but I will see you again, and your heart will rejoice, and no one will take your joy away from you. (John 16:20–22 WEB)

In the end of times, the Bible talks about a great tribulation—an apocalyptic idea of the birth pangs during the holy wars, the suffering of God's people (Christians)—but will be replaced with the joy of the return of Jesus called the second coming.

> For nation will rise against nation, and kingdom against kingdom; and there will be famines, plagues, and earthquakes in various places. But all these things are the beginning of birth pains… This Good News of the Kingdom will be preached in the whole world for a testimony to all the nations, and then the end will come. (Matthew 24:7–8; 14 WEB)

God gave us life, then after the original sin, caused travail—birthing pains. Jesus's death accomplished a new birth and a hope that lies beyond sorrow. After the end of times when Satan attacks, causing travail and suffering, Christians know that joy will cometh. Christ will prove His deity in His second coming and will bring eternal life to all his chosen. All these transitions will have travail, but joy cometh.

> For I consider that the sufferings of this present time are not worthy to be compared with the glory which will be revealed toward us. (Romans 8:18 WEB)

ESCHATOLOGY

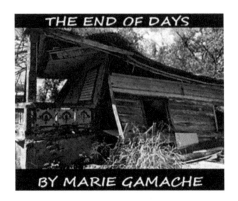

THE END OF DAYS

BY MARIE GAMACHE

Eschatology is the theory of the final events in human history, end times, death, judgment, and the final destiny of our souls. It will be the end of this reality as we know it and for humans to be reborn in the presence of our Lord and to be able to see God face-to-face.

Human history is divided into time periods. One age comes to an end, and then a new era begins a new time period. There is a change in the environment, a new way of living, and a new level of consciousness. When God had Noah build an ark because God was going to flood the earth to abolish evil people, a new life was to begin. When God led the Israelites through the deserts, they came out with a new idea on life; and when Jesus came, His crucifixion and resurrection started a whole new beginning for us. It was a struggle for new Christians to survive the persecutions of the Roman Empire, but it provided the prophetic fulfillment of a final course in history.

Now Christians are waiting for the return of Jesus, the resurrection of the dead, tribulation, the last judgment, a new heaven and a new earth, and the ultimate consummation of God come to fruition.

Daniel's Prophecy of the End Times

"At that time Michael will stand up, the great prince who stands for the children of your people; and there will be a time of trouble, such as never was since there was a nation even to that same time. At that time your people will be delivered, everyone who is found written in the book. Many of those who sleep in the dust of the earth will awake, some to everlasting life, and some to shame and everlasting contempt. Those who are wise will shine as the brightness of the expanse. Those who turn many to righteousness will shine as the stars forever and ever. But you, Daniel, shut up the words, and seal the book, even to the time of the end. Many will run back and forth, and knowledge will be increased."

Then I, Daniel, looked, and behold, two others stood, one on the riverbank on this side, and the other on the riverbank on that side. One said to the man clothed in linen, who was above the waters of the river, "How long will it be to the end of these wonders?"

I heard the man clothed in linen, who was above the waters of the river, when he held up his right hand and his left hand to heaven, and swore by him who lives forever that it will be for a time, times, and a half; and when they have finished breaking in pieces the power of the holy people, all these things will be finished.

I heard, but I didn't understand. Then I said, "My lord, what will be the outcome of these things?"

He said, "Go your way, Daniel; for the words are shut up and sealed until the time of the end. Many will purify themselves, and make themselves white, and be refined; but the wicked will do wickedly; and none of the wicked will understand; but those who are wise will understand.

"From the time that the continual burnt offering is taken away, and the abomination that makes desolate set up, there will be one thousand two hundred ninety days. Blessed is he who waits and comes to the one thousand three hundred thirty-five days.

"But go your way until the end; for you will rest and will stand in your inheritance at the end of the days." (Daniel 12:1–13 WEB)

A TRUE VISIONARY

The Apostle John was a true visionary leader. He grew up in Bethsaida with his father Zebedee who was a wealthy fisherman on the Sea of Galilee. He and his brother, James, were normal, very active brothers, strong, robust, and full of character. A couple of vigorous youngsters that would one day become disciples for Jesus. Because of their unique characters, Jesus soon nicknamed them "sons of thunder."

> And Simon he surnamed Peter; And James the son of Zebedee, and John the brother of James; and he surnamed them Boanerges, which is, The sons of thunder:" (Mark 3:16–17 KJV)

Over the years the reality of Jesus Christ deepened in John's heart, he soon became the most beloved disciple. John could understand Jesus in a way that no one else could. Every time Jesus would talk about His Father in heaven, John would have these incredible dreams and visions, and then he would write about them as if they were understood crystal clear, visions of the past, present, and the future. He revealed that Jesus was God in creative ways.

> In the beginning was the Word, and the Word was with God, and the Word was God. The same was in the beginning with God. All things were made by him; and without him was

not anything made that was made. In him was life; and the life was the light of men. And the light shineth in darkness; and the darkness comprehended it not. (John 1:1–5 KJV)

It is John who intercepts the Trinity, the ultimate message that Jesus Christ is God himself and the Holy Spirit is both. He traces Jesus all the way back to the beginning of time, as God Himself. He portrays Jesus in His deity as the Son of Man, was the Word of God, creator of Heaven and Earth, the bearer of light and human life. John also grasps the meaning of eschatology, end of days and the second coming of our Lord Jesus Christ, and writes the last book in the Bible, Revelation.

After the crucifixion of Jesus, anyone who proclaimed Him as the messiah was persecuted. John lived more than half a century after the martyrdom of his brother, James, who was the first apostle to die a martyr's death. Emperor Nero had John taken to Rome for trial, and he was sentenced to death for confessing his faith in Christ. John was forced to drink a cup of deadly poison, but he remained alive. Later, he was thrown into a cauldron of boiling oil and emerged unharmed. Christ preserved His Beloved chosen one.

After Nero's death, John was banished to the Island of Patmos during the reign of the new emperor, Domitian. John was freed after Domitian's death and was the only apostle who lived out his natural life. Christ preserved John through the excruciating pains of torture. I can just imagine him in a deep trance receiving an apparition from Christ, taking him to a different place, a beautiful place, a place more powerful than anyone could imagine.

It's no wonder that he was called the beloved disciple; not even Satan could get into his mind and under his skin. That is what we need to do. Not let Satan in our minds and tell us that our cravings for material things are more important than our soul! We are so desperately looking for something that we forget to believe in ourselves and stop searching for the Christ within us. So go ahead and dream the impossible dreams and let God show you His kingdom, and you, too, can become a true visionary for Christ.

CHAPTER 1

The Book of Revelation

A REFERENCE CHART

The Bible is full of images that are symbolic to understanding Revelation. Here is a chart of numbers, colors, animals, and other symbols that will help you unlock their meaning:

Numbers

1: God Himself, absolute singleness, greatness (Deuteronomy 6:4).

2: Witness and support: When two or more are gathered in My name (Luke 10:1).

3: Unity, completion and perfection: The Trinity.

4: Earth with four seasons, cosmos in four directions: North, south, east and west.

5: Grace: Jesus multiplied five loaves of bread to feed five thousand (Matthew 14:17)

6: The number of man. Adam and Eve were created on the sixth day (Genesis 1:31); it also means imperfection.

7: Devine perfection, completion, covenant. Mary Magdalene had seven demons that went out from her symbolizing total deliverance (Luke 8:2).

8: New beginnings.

9: Fullness of blessing; there are nine fruits of the spirit (Galatians 5:22–23).

10: Shortness, limitations such as the Ten Commandments, Gods laws (Exodus 20:1–17).

12: Continuity, the twelve tribes, the twelve apostles.

30: A time given to mourn or be sorrowful.

40: A period of testing and trials.

50: Celebrations and ceremonies, such as Pentecost.

70: Judgment and human delegations. Seventy elders were appointed by Moses (Numbers 11:16). Israel spent seventy years in Babylonian captivity (Jeremiah 29:10).

666: The number of the beast (Revelation 13:13–18).

144,000: 12x12x1,000—represents all of God's people in union with him (Revelation 14:1–5). The Twelve tribes Israel (Revelation 7:4–10).

Colors

White: Purity, victory, dignity.
Black: Death, distress, disaster.
Red: Bloodshed, violence.
Green: Means pale, impending death.
Scarlet: Means blood. Color of sin or immorality.
Purple: Royalty, majesty, wealth, prosperity, peace, pride.

Animals

Beasts: Foreign nations against God's people.
Dragon or Serpent: Satan, Lucifer.
Eagle, Lion, Man, Ox: Four of the mightiest creatures.
Lamb: Jesus.

Other Symbols

Amen: Means to believe, truth, trustworthiness and faithfulness to God and His faithfulness to us.
Babylon: Exile, loss of freedom.
Crown: Authority.
Egypt: Oppressor of God's people.
Full of Eyes: All seeing, all knowing power.
Hades or Sheol: The underworld, hell, or a place of the dead.
Horns: Power.
Jewels: Precious, rare, and unique.
Key of David: The power to open or shut God's kingdom.
Lampstands: Churches.
Left hand: Cursed, separation, unclean, justice for the unfaithful.
Palm branches: Victory or joy. The waving of palm branches on Palm Sunday (Mark 11:9–10).

Right hand: Power and authority, mercy in the right hand of God.

Seals, trumpets, bowls: These are liturgical images for repentance and to announce the dispense of judgment.

Sodom: Immorality.

Spirits, stars, winds, or horsemen: Angels.

Thunder or loud booming sound: God's voice, represents His authority, sovereignty, power, glory, and majesty.

End Times: The world events that will reach a climax before the apocalypse.

The Second Coming: When Christ returns to earth.

Rapture: When Christ transports believers from earth to heaven.

Armageddon: The final battle between good and evil on earth, where Christ defeats Satan and Satan's followers.

Tribulation: A seven-year period when God completes His discipline to unbelievers and makes His final judgment.

Apocalypse: The unveiling of the final destruction of the world.

THE SECOND COMING

The Book of Revelation is a revelation of Jesus Christ. It brings our future into focus. Just as Genesis is the book of the beginning, Revelation is the book of the end. In it is God's divine program of redemption before all creation. God's justified plans brought to fruition.

The word *revelation* in Greek is *apokalypsis*, which means "pull back the veil or the covers, unveiling, uncovering, or disclosure." In Scripture, it is referring to a sacred bridal chamber of the Lord and his bride, the church.

> As a bridegroom rejoices over his bride,
> so your God will rejoice over you. (Isaiah 62:5
> WEB)

One could say that God is a romantic.

The book was penned by the Apostle John during his exile on the Island of Patmos on AD 70. These letters were treated as sacred scriptures, divinely inspired, because immediately after hearing the words or reading them, you are blessed and consecrated by God. It even says that in the first passage.

This is the Revelation of Jesus Christ, which God gave him to show to his servants the things which must happen soon, which he sent and made known by his angel to his servant, John, who testified to God's word and of the testimony of Jesus Christ, about everything that he saw. Blessed is he who reads and those who hear the words of the prophecy, and keep the things that are written in it, for the time is at hand. (Revelation 1:1–3 WEB)

There are many interesting images woven into this book, and I hope to uncover their meaning and relevance. Christians are now living out the last epoch in history, the final days. The second coming of Jesus Christ will be a glorified time for His people. God will bring us to our glorified new bodies, dress us in white, crown our heads, and we will see Jesus rejoicing because we will be seeing Him face-to-face. Christ will raise up the dead first—all those who crucified Him, mocked Him; all His Saints and believers, the good and the bad: all eyes will see Him. There will be a revelation for everyone: that Jesus is God and that He has come. We are never without His sight.

Therefore prepare your minds for action. Be sober, and set your hope fully on the grace that will be brought to you at the revelation of Jesus Christ—as children of obedience, not conforming yourselves according to your former lusts as in your ignorance, but just as he who called you is holy, you yourselves also be holy in all of your behavior; because it is written, "You shall be holy; for I am holy." If you call on him as Father, who without respect of persons judges according to each man's work, pass the time of your living as foreigners here in reverent fear, knowing that you were redeemed, not with corruptible things, with silver or gold, from the useless way of life handed down from your fathers, but with precious blood, as of a lamb without blemish or spot, the blood of Christ, who was foreknown indeed before the foundation of the world, but was revealed in this last age for your sake, who through him are believers in God, who raised him from the dead, and gave him glory, so that your faith and hope might be in God. (1 Peter 1:13–21 WEB) (See reference: Leviticus 11:44–45)

This is an obvious sign of the righteous judgment of God, to the end that you may be counted worthy of God's Kingdom, for which you also suffer. Since it is a righteous thing with God to repay affliction to those who afflict you, and to give relief to you who are afflicted with us, when the Lord Jesus is revealed from heaven with his mighty angels in flaming fire, punishing those who don't know God, and to those who don't obey the Good News of our Lord Jesus, who will pay the penalty: eternal destruction from the face of the Lord and from the glory of his might, when he comes in that day to be glorified in his saints and to be admired among all those who have believed, because our testimony to you was believed. To this end we also pray always for you, that our God may count you worthy of your calling, and fulfill every desire of goodness and work of faith with power, that the name of our Lord Jesus may be glorified in you, and you in him, according to the grace of our God and the Lord Jesus Christ." (2 Thessalonians 1:5–12 WEB)

When this second coming will occur, is when God decides the fullness of time.

to proclaim the year of Yahweh's favor and
the day of vengeance of our God, to comfort all
who mourn. (Isaiah 61:2 WEB)

making known to us the mystery of his will,
according to his good pleasure which he pur-
posed in him to an administration of the fullness
of the times, to sum up all things in Christ, the
things in the heavens and the things on the earth,
in him. (Ephesians 1:9–10 WEB)

To sum up all things means to recap everyone's time spent.
Sister Regina, my spiritual director, said that we will be asked how
we spent our time in Christ. How often and how much did we love
others? Throughout the history of humanity, all matter of sin has
taken place. There have been many wars in history, holocaust, and
mass exterminations.

Genocide is the worst crime against humanity; it is the deliber-
ate destruction, in whole or in part, of an ethnic, racial, religious, or
national group of people. The Holocaust in Germany, by the Nazi
government, killed some six million European Jews in twelve years,
between 1933 and 1945. This did not just kill people: it challenged
spirituality and the way people think about God.

Mao Zedong the Chinese communist emerges as one of the
greatest tales of horror, murdering forty million people in four years,
between 1958 and 1962. If you think that forty million people exter-
minated in four years is a lot, well think again. Abortion is the delib-
erate termination of a human, any and all humans within an ethnic,
racial, religious, national—all of humanity. Abortion worldwide is
estimated killing fifty million babies (God's precious gifts) each year!
That is 125,000 babies being killed each day!

There are destructive tendencies still lurking within humanity.
It is in these destructive actions that is a misuse of human power. This
freedom that God gives us must be stopped and channeled toward
our transcending and compelling God. At one point in time, God
will decide that we can sin no more. When God decides that we have

committed all sins possible and no more sins can take place, we will have reached the limit, the fullness of time. Humanity will have hit rock bottom, I say, and the only way from there is up; the only other way to go from the bottom is to the top.

It is in this manner that God will know that the people left for heaven bound will be able to live eternally without sinning. He must be sure that heaven is never corrupted. Anyone who does not believe in Jesus will perish. Jesus will be our judge, and vengeance is for our God because we had all the time in the world to figure out how much our wonderful and compelling God loves us. May God have mercy on our souls. Amen.

DOXOLOGY

The word *doxology* in Greek means "glory." It is to express praise and glory to God, either in written or oral form. As we read these next passages, we will discover that Jesus is referring this glory to God as glory to Himself. Christ is the one who is and who was and who is to come, the faithful witness, the firstborn of the dead, and the ruler of the kings of the earth. We must take this to heart that every blessing that has been promised will be completed.

John, to the seven assemblies that are in Asia: Grace to you and peace from God, who is and who was and who is to come; and from the seven Spirits who are before his throne; and from Jesus Christ, the faithful witness, the first-born of the dead, and the ruler of the kings of the earth. To him who loves us, and washed us from our sins by his blood—and he made us to be a Kingdom, priests to his God and Father—to him be the glory and the dominion forever and ever. Amen. Behold, he is coming with the clouds, and every eye will see him, including those who pierced him. All the tribes of the earth will mourn over him. Even so, Amen. "I am the Alpha and the Omega," says the Lord God, "who is and who was and who is to come, the Almighty." (Revelation 1:4–8 WEB) (See reference: Exodus 19:6; Isaiah 61:6)

God said to Moses, "I AM WHO I AM," and he said, "You shall tell the children of Israel this: 'I AM has sent me to you.'" (Exodus 3:14 WEB)

But you are a chosen race, a royal priesthood, a holy nation, a people for God's own possession, that you may proclaim the excellence of him who called you out of darkness into his marvelous light. (1 Peter 2:9 WEB)

He is the head of the body, the assembly, who is the beginning, the firstborn from the dead, that in all things he might have the preeminence. (Colossians 1:18 WEB)

"And you shall be to me a kingdom of priests and a holy nation.' These are the words which you shall speak to the children of Israel." (Exodus 19:6 WEB)

But you will be called Yahweh's priests. Men will call you the servants of our God. You will eat the wealth of the nations. You will boast in their glory. (Isaiah 61:6 WEB)

Jesus told John to write letters to the seven churches of Asia which are Ephesus, Smyrna, Pergamum, Thyatira, Sardis, Philadelphia, and Laodicea. These are the first churches established for Christ at that time. The number seven signifies completion or covenant. The seven spirits are going to build Christ a new glorious kingdom. Jesus is proclaiming that He alone will be the high priest and the ruler of the earth, all dressed in a white garment with a gold band and brass boots. White is a symbol for victory, purity, and dignity. These churches were facing persecutions from the emperor and facing many tribulations and needed their savior's encouragement.

In the second coming, Christ will be addressing all His churches and all people. Even now, two thousand years later, Jesus encourages us to be faithful and busy little beavers for Him because, He will come again to judge the living and the dead and his kingdom will have no end. You will see your God face to face.

I COME IN PEACE

We all know that Christ came in peace.

> Peace I leave with you. My peace I give to you; not as the world gives, I give to you. Don't let your heart be troubled, neither let it be fearful. (John 14:27, WEB).

We also know that Christ came to have his chosen apostles establish Christian churches. There were so many Greek gods in those days that Christ needed parishes that would only worship the one true God. By the time John was in exile, there were seven churches established in the seven largest cities in Asia. One in Ephesus, Smyrna, Pergamum, Thyatira, Sardis, Philadelphia, and Laodicea. But because of the many different cultures blending many different gods, some of the Christians faded away to Nicolaism, the worship of Balaam, resulting in many Christians fading away from Christ's teaching, while others stayed faithful to the one true God. These churches were only about thirty years old when Christ came to John on the island of Patmos.

In these next passages, Christ is announcing that He will make a speech to each of the seven churches. He needed to address their unfaithfulness and give confirmation to His faithful. Christ was aware of their moral apathy. Some lacked motivation that could carry a seed of destruction. The lampstands are the churches or assemblies. Christ spoke in a loud voice like a trumpet. The symbol for trumpet or horn is power.

> I turned to see the voice that spoke with me. Having turned, I saw seven golden lamp stands. And among the lamp stands was one like a son of man, clothed with a robe reaching down to his feet, and with a golden sash around his chest. His head and his hair were white as white wool, like snow. His eyes were like a flame of fire. His feet were like burnished brass, as if it had been refined in a furnace. His voice was like the voice of many waters. He had seven stars in his right hand. Out of his mouth proceeded a sharp two-edged sword. His face was like the sun shining at its brightest. When I saw him, I fell at his feet like a dead man. He laid his right hand on me, saying, "Don't be afraid. I am the first and the last, and the Living one. I was dead, and behold, I am alive forever and ever. Amen. I have the keys of Death and of Hades. Write therefore the things which you have seen, and the things which are, and the things which will happen hereafter. The mystery of the seven stars which you saw in my right hand, and the seven golden lamp stands is this: The seven stars are the angels of the seven assemblies. The seven lamp stands are seven assemblies. (Revelation 1:12–20 WEB) (See reference: Daniel 7:13)

> "I saw in the night visions, and behold, there came with the clouds of the sky one like a son of man, and he came even to the ancient of days, and they brought him near before him." (Daniel 7:13 WEB)

EPHESUS

Ephesus was the fourth largest and most impressive city in the ancient world. Its population was estimated at 250,000 people. Politically, Ephesus was the unofficial capital of the Roman province of Asia. Located at the mouth of the Cayster River and situated between the Maeander River to the south and the Hermus River to the north. It was a commercial seaport, had political power, and the city played a significant role in the early spread of Christianity. The library of Celsus was made to hold twelve thousand scrolls and a theater that seated twenty-four thousand. It even had terrace housing with hot and cold running water, gymnasiums, and public baths. The streets were well laid throughout the city and colossal statues of the emperor Domitian. The original temple of Artemis was in Ephesus and was one of the Seven Wonders of the Ancient World.

The Ephesian Christians rejected the false apostles, Nicolaitans—a term meaning "overcome the people"—and also rejected Queen Jezebel who practiced the worship of Balaam. The Book of Ephesians is an epistle, a letter that Paul wrote to the Ephesians. It includes one of the best sets of the basic concepts of the Christian faith.

"To the angel of the assembly in Ephesus write:

"He who holds the seven stars in his right hand, he who walks among the seven golden lamp stands says these things:

"I know your works, and your toil and perseverance, and that you can't tolerate evil men, and have tested those who call themselves apostles, and they are not, and found them false. You have perseverance and have endured for my name's sake and have not grown weary. But I have this against you, that you left your first love. Remember therefore from where you have fallen, and repent and do the first works; or else I am coming to you swiftly and will move your lamp stand out of its place, unless you repent. But this you have, that you hate the works of the Nicolaitans, which I also hate. He who has an ear, let him hear what the Spirit says to the assemblies. To him who overcomes I will give to eat from the tree of life, which is in the Paradise of my God." (Revelation 2:1–7 WEB)

SMYRNA

Smyrna was the most beautiful city along the Aegean coast. It was referred to as the crown of Smyrna. The city was at the foot of Mount Pagus and at the outlet of the Hermus River, allowing extensive trade to pass through the city. It held Olympian games, had stately public buildings, and the city spread outward on the sloping hill sides. In AD 178, an earthquake destroyed the city.

Under the reign of Domitian, the people of Smyrna were required to burn incense on the altar to Caesar. Christians were threatened to be thrown into prison for refusing to worship Caesar. Polycarp was the bishop of Smyrna; he was, at one time, a disciple of the Apostle John's before his exile to Patmos. John ordained Polycarp as bishop. He was one of the first martyrs of the church for his faith in Christ in AD 155.

Christ knew of the poverty and afflictions that the people of Smyrna were facing. Some Christians were claiming to be Jews but were not, and John called this Jewish opposition a synagogue of Satan. Nonetheless, Christ encourages this church to remain faithful until their death, and He will give them a victor's crown.

> "To the angel of the assembly in Smyrna write:
> "The first and the last, who was dead, and has come to life says these things:
> "I know your works, oppression, and your poverty (but you are rich), and the blasphemy of those who say they are Jews, and they are not, but are a synagogue of Satan. Don't be afraid of the

things which you are about to suffer. Behold, the devil is about to throw some of you into prison, that you may be tested; and you will have oppression for ten days. Be faithful to death, and I will give you the crown of life. He who has an ear, let him hear what the Spirit says to the assemblies. He who overcomes won't be harmed by the second death." (Revelation 2:8–11 WEB)

PERGAMUM

Pergamum is called "Satan's throne" or "where Satan lives" because the people practiced paganism cults and proudly called themselves "guardians of the imperial cult." Pergamum was built on a hill, one thousand feet high, and was sixteen miles from the Aegean Sea. It was famous for its health spas and medical centers with accomplished physicians. Ancient Pergamum was a wealthy city in Asia Minor but is now the site of Bergama, Turkey.

Pergamum was home to a library said to house approximate two hundred thousand scrolls. Built by King Eumenes II, it became one of the most important libraries in the ancient world. The library was the second largest library. The largest library was The Great Library of Alexandria in Egypt that held four hundred thousand scrolls. Manuscripts were written on parchment, rolled, and then stored on these shelves.

Pergamum is credited with being the home and namesake of parchment (*charta pergamena*). Prior to the creation of parchment, manuscripts were transcribed on papyrus, which was produced only in Alexandria, Egypt. When the Ptolemies refused to export any more papyrus to Pergamum, King Eumenes II commanded that an alternative source be found. By simplifying the pelt bath preparation and drying the wet pelts by stretching them as much as possible, it gave a smooth taut sheet that could be erased and used again. This led to the production of parchment and reduced the Roman Empire's dependency on Egyptian papyrus.

Faithful Christians in Pergamum, who overcame the Balaamites or Nicolaitans, will be provided hidden manna, a white stone, and a new name. When Christ returns, he will provide manna for the righteous so they don't eat the meat offered to idols. The white stone is given to replace the required magical amulet to be worn for entrance into the banquets held in pagan temples. These magical amulets were to have been said to ward off evil spirits, and they were often white. The front side of the amulet or coin was the image of a deity of the temple, and on the other side, the back side of the amulet, was a secret name of the worshiper; this was hidden from view. The white stone Christ gives to His faithful Christians will have a new name written on it, which no one knows; but he who receives it, the secret name of their worshiper is Christ.

"To the angel of the assembly in Pergamum write:

"He who has the sharp two-edged sword says these things:

"I know your works and where you dwell, where Satan's throne is. You hold firmly to my name and didn't deny my faith in the days of Antipas my witness, my faithful one, who was killed among you, where Satan dwells. But I have a few things against you, because you have there some who hold the teaching of Balaam, who taught Balak to throw a stumbling block before the children of Israel, to eat things sacrificed to idols, and to commit sexual immorality. So, you also have some who hold to the teaching of the Nicolaitans likewise. Repent therefore, or else I am coming to you quickly, and I will make war against them with the sword of my mouth. He who has an ear, let him hear what the Spirit says to the assemblies. To him who overcomes, to him I will give of the hidden manna, and I will give him a white stone, and on the stone a new name written, which no one knows but he who receives it." (Revelation 2:12–17 WEB)

THYATIRA

Thyatira was an ancient city in the Lycus River Valley in western Asia Minor but is now modern-day Turkey. There were three gymnasiums that held gladiator schools and were most notable for their guild trade association of craftsmen and merchants. Shoemakers, bronze smiths, wool workers, and the making of purple-dyed cloths. Purple is the symbol for immorality, and bronze is the symbol for strength and durability. Christ addresses to them that He is the Son of God, not Apollo, the son of Zeus, Artemis, Helius, or Caesar. His eyes are like a fiery flame, and feet like burnished brass or bronze; these images are relevant to the metalworking trade.

The church at Thyatira was praised for its works in charity, service, and their faith as followers of Christ. They rejected the followers of Jezebel—the wicked queen of Israel, wife of King Ahab, and daughter of Ithobaal, King of Sidon. She was the teacher of Balaamite or Nicolaitan cult. The bed of suffering will be judged to Satan's so-called deep secrets. The overcomers will be blessed by Christ.

> "To the angel of the assembly in Thyatira write:
> "The Son of God, who has his eyes like a flame of fire, and his feet are like burnished brass, says these things:

"I know your works, your love, faith, service, patient endurance, and that your last works are more than the first. But I have this against you, that you tolerate your woman, Jezebel, who calls herself a prophetess. She teaches and seduces my servants to commit sexual immorality, and to eat things sacrificed to idols. I gave her time to repent, but she refuses to repent of her sexual immorality. Behold, I will throw her and those who commit adultery with her into a bed of great oppression, unless they repent of her works. I will kill her children with Death, and all the assemblies will know that I am he who searches the minds and hearts. I will give to each one of you according to your deeds. But to you I say, to the rest who are in Thyatira, as many as don't have this teaching, who don't know what some call 'the deep things of Satan,' to you I say, I am not putting any other burden on you. Nevertheless, hold that which you have firmly until I come. He who overcomes, and he who keeps my works to the end, to him I will give authority over the nations. He will rule them with a rod of iron, shattering them like clay pots; as I also have received of my Father: and I will give him the morning star. He who has an ear, let him hear what the Spirit says to the assemblies." (Revelation 2:18–29 WEB) (See reference: Psalm 2:9)

You shall break them with a rod of iron. You shall dash them in pieces like a potter's vessel. (Psalm 2:9 WEB)

SARDIS

Sardis's natural barriers ensured its safety for hundreds of years, surrounded on three sides by a fifteen-hundred-foot precipice and a steep approach on the south side on the slope of Mount Tmolus. Because it was on a major trade route, its economy was rich with clothes and jewelry shops, a bath-gymnasium facility on five acres of land, and many games originated there. They were the first to mint gold and silver coins, and they had learned of a technique to dye wool. The famous spring from the Pactolus River was full of gold. Some used to say that Midas, the mythological Phrygian king, bathed the river to eliminate the gold with his Midas touch.

Sardis had the largest Jewish synagogue in the land of Israel; it held about one thousand worshipers, but the church was condemned as being dead because it was ineffective to the world. One of the major temples was of Artemis, the goddess of love and fertility. Artemis and Cybele were the patron deities of the city, and Christ warns them to change their ways and demands that the Christians wake up and repent.

"And to the angel of the assembly in Sardis write:
"He who has the seven Spirits of God and the seven stars says these things:
"I know your works, that you have a reputation of being alive, but you are dead. Wake up and keep the things that remain, which you were about to throw away, for I have found no works

of yours perfected before my God. Remember therefore how you have received and heard. Keep it and repent. If therefore you won't watch, I will come as a thief, and you won't know what hour I will come upon you. Nevertheless, you have a few names in Sardis that didn't defile their garments. They will walk with me in white, for they are worthy. He who overcomes will be arrayed in white garments, and I will in no way blot his name out of the book of life, and I will confess his name before my Father, and before his angels. He who has an ear, let him hear what the Spirit says to the assemblies." (Revelation 3:1–6 WEB)

PHILADELPHIA

Philadelphia means "love of brother," and the church held the key of David. This is referring to what the prophet Isaiah said about the Lord replacing Shebna with a man named Eliakim. Eliakim was a gatekeeper to the royal kingdom and decided who could or could not have access to the king.

> It will happen in that day that I will call my servant Eliakim the son of Hilkiah, and I will clothe him with your robe, and strengthen him with your belt. I will commit your government into his hand; and he will be a father to the inhabitants of Jerusalem, and to the house of Judah. I will lay the key of David's house on his shoulder. He will open, and no one will shut. He will shut, and no one will open. I will fasten him like a nail in a sure place. He will be for a throne of glory to his father's house. (Isaiah 20–23 WEB)

The Jewish Christians believed that Jesus was the Messiah, attended the church worship, and read from Hebrew Scriptures as their Bible. Jesus says for them to hold firmly that which they have done, preaching the gospels to the whole world, because it is their salvation and their access to the kingdom of God.

Some of the people proclaimed to be Jewish but were not; they were persecuting the Christian, saying that Jesus was not the

Messiah. Jesus called these Jews "synagogue of Satan," and eventually they came to know the truth about Jesus and changed their ways.

Christ promised the faithful that he would make them pillars in God's temple.

> "To the angel of the assembly in Philadelphia write:
>
> "He who is holy, he who is true, he who has the key of David, he who opens, and no one can shut, and who shuts and no one opens, says these things:
>
> "I know your works (behold, I have set before you an open door, which no one can shut), that you have a little power, and kept my word, and didn't deny my name. Behold, I give some of the synagogue of Satan, of those who say they are Jews, and they are not, but lie—behold, I will make them to come and worship before your feet, and to know that I have loved you. Because you kept my command to endure, I also will keep you from the hour of testing, which is to come on the whole world, to test those who dwell on the earth. I am coming quickly! Hold firmly that which you have, so that no one takes your crown. He who overcomes, I will make him a pillar in the temple of my God, and he will go out from there no more. I will write on him the name of my God and the name of the city of my God, the new Jerusalem, which comes down out of heaven from my God, and my own new name. He who has an ear, let him hear what the Spirit says to the assemblies." (Revelation 3:7–13 WEB)

LAODICEA

Laodicea was founded by the Seleucid King Antiochus II who named the city after his divorced wife Laodice. It was located in two trade routes which made the people wealthy, it became a banking center, producer of black wool for garments, and had a famous school of medicine that discovered Phrygian powder for an eye salve.

The church was spiritually naked because the wealthy people did not need anything from Christ. Their pride was counselled by Christ to apply a spiritual eye salve so they could see that they have fallen into blindness. Their white garments were a symbol of righteousness, but they cannot gain righteousness through their own efforts: only Christ can remove impurities of the human soul.

Laodicea had no water supply; the nearest spring was five miles away, and by the time the piped water reached the city, it was tepid and emetic, causing vomiting. Antiochus IV was known as a madman, and some scholars believe this is due to the poor water supply.

> And many Israelites delighted in his religion; they sacrificed to idols and profaned the sabbath.
>
> The king sent letters by messenger to Jerusalem and to the cities of Judah, ordering them to follow customs foreign to their land; to prohibit burnt offerings, sacrifices, and liba-

tions in the sanctuary, to profane the sabbaths and feast days, to desecrate the sanctuary and the sacred ministers, to build pagan altars and temples and shrines, to sacrifice swine and unclean animals, to leave their sons uncircumcised, and to defile themselves with every kind of impurity and abomination; so that they might forget the law and change all its ordinances. Whoever refused to act according to the command of the king was to be put to death.

In words such as these he wrote to his whole kingdom. He appointed inspectors over all the people, and he ordered the cities of Judah to offer sacrifices, each city in turn. Many of the people, those who abandoned the law, joined them and committed evil in the land. (1 Maccabees 1:43–52 NABRE)

"To the angel of the assembly in Laodicea write:

"The Amen, the Faithful and True Witness, the Beginning of God's creation, says these things:

"I know your works, that you are neither cold nor hot. I wish you were cold or hot. So, because you are lukewarm, and neither hot nor cold, I will vomit you out of my mouth. Because you say, 'I am rich, and have gotten riches, and have need of nothing;' and don't know that you are the wretched one, miserable, poor, blind, and naked; I counsel you to buy from me gold refined by fire, that you may become rich; and white garments, that you may clothe yourself, and that the shame of your nakedness may not be revealed; and eye salve to anoint your eyes, that you may see. As many as I love, I reprove and chasten. Be zealous therefore, and repent. Behold, I stand at the door and knock. If anyone hears my voice and opens the door, then I will come in, to him, and will dine with him, and he with me. He who overcomes, I will give to him to sit down with me on my throne, as I also overcame, and sat down with my Father on his throne. He who has an ear, let him hear what the Spirit says to the assemblies." (Revelation 3:14–22 WEB)

QUEEN JEZEBEL

Queen Jezebel was married to King Ahab of Israel during his reign 871–852 BC. Jezebel was the most wicked queen known because she forced the people to worship Baal, a fertility god of ancient cultures. Her name in Hebrew means "chaste" or "where is the prince?". Jezebel persuaded Ahab to build an altar to honor and worship Baal inside God's sacred temple in Samaria. She also forced people to eat the animals that were sacrificed. Jezebel was the daughter of the Phoenician priest-king Ithobaal.

> But I have this against you, that you tolerate your woman, Jezebel, who calls herself a prophetess. She teaches and seduces my servants to commit sexual immorality, and to eat things sacrificed to idols. (Revelation 2:20 WEB)

She devised a sequence of events to have all of Yahweh's prophets destroyed, but God had His prophet, Elijah, call down fire from heaven and slaughter hundreds of Jezebel's false prophets.

> Elijah went to show himself to Ahab. The famine was severe in Samaria. Ahab called Obadiah, who was over the household. (Now Obadiah feared Yahweh greatly; for when Jezebel

cut off Yahweh's prophets, Obadiah took one hundred prophets, and hid them fifty to a cave, and fed them with bread and water.) (1 Kings 18:2–4 WEB)

Elijah said to them, "Seize the prophets of Baal! Don't let one of them escape!" (1 Kings 18:40 WEB)

Ahab told Jezebel all that Elijah had done, and how he had killed all the prophets with the sword. (1 Kings 19:1 WEB)

Elijah prophesied that Jezebel would fall to her death and get eaten by dogs.

Yahweh also spoke of Jezebel, saying, "The dogs will eat Jezebel by the rampart of Jezreel." (1 Kings 21:23 WEB)

When Jehu had come to Jezreel, Jezebel heard of it; and she painted her eyes, and adorned her head, and looked out at the window. As Jehu entered in at the gate, she said, "Do you come in peace, Zimri, you murderer of your master?"

He lifted up his face to the window, and said, "Who is on my side? Who?"

Two or three eunuchs looked out at him.

He said, "Throw her down!"

So they threw her down; and some of her blood was sprinkled on the wall, and on the horses. Then he trampled her under foot. When he had come in, he ate and drank. Then he said, "See now to this cursed woman, and bury her; for she is a king's daughter."

They went to bury her, but they found no more of her than the skull, the feet, and the palms of her hands. Therefore they came back, and told him.

He said, "This is Yahweh's word, which he spoke by his servant Elijah the Tishbite, saying, 'The dogs will eat the flesh of Jezebel on the plot of Jezreel, and the body of Jezebel will be as dung on the face of the field on Jezreel's land, so that they won't say, "This is Jezebel."'" (2 Kings 9:30–37 WEB)

Jezebel was intelligent and knew how to influence people. Even today, when someone knows a woman who is selfish, deceitful, and manipulative, they nickname her "Jezebel."

THE CHURCH ERA

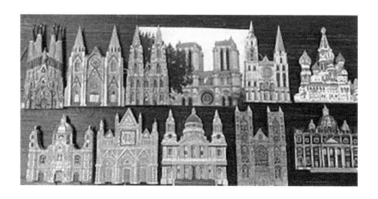

The church era is the history that characterizes the service of and for Jesus Christ and identifying it through the works of the churches. The first church was the Roman Catholic. The Apostle Peter, who Jesus called the rock, was the first Roman Catholic pope.

> I also tell you that you are Peter, and on this rock, I will build my assembly, and the gates of Hades will not prevail against it. (Matthew 16:18 WEB)

Jesus told Peter to build the church with a solid rock foundation, and that is just what he did.

The word *Catholic* means "unity," and every cathedral around the world is Catholic. *Cathedral* means "seat of the bishop." In the Vatican in Rome, Italy, there is a giant chair called the Chair of Saint Peter. It represents the Chair of Moses's from the Old Testament, known as the judgment seat. Every Catholic mass around the world has the same mass presided each day at each church; this represents the unity of the Catholic faith. The teachings of the Catholic faith are through *catechism*—it means "to echo." We are taught to echo, to pass onto others what we learn about Jesus through the priests and his congregation. This corporate idea of worship is passed on from the teachings in the Bible. Revelation is the key to the liturgy, the kingdom yet to come.

"Holy, holy, holy, Lord God Almighty, who was and who is and who is to come!" (Revelation 4:8 WEB)

"Behold, the Lamb of God, who takes away the sin of the world!" (John 1:29 WEB)

My favorite song is the Eucharistic prayer, "Holy, holy, holy, Lord God of hosts. Heaven and earth are full of your glory. Hosanna in the highest." Every time we sing it, my skin feels prickly, like goosebumps all over. I think it is the Holy Spirit bearing witness that Jesus is our Messiah and our God.

In a Christian church is exactly where you will find this strong foundation of teaching to keep you on good terms with Jesus and to keep you out of trouble.

Blessed are the meek: for they shall inherit the earth. (Matthew 5:5 ASV)

Wait for Yahweh, and keep his way, and he will exalt you to inherit the land. When the wicked are cut off, you shall see it. (Psalm 37:34 WEB)

Going to church gives us a chance to rest and offer prayers and charity to others in need. It is the house of God for worship and to set aside private time to thank Him for everything. It is important for us to deepen our communion with God. God's love will move so subtly through us that His love will echo and reflect onto others.

And above all things be earnest in your love among yourselves, for love covers a multitude of sins. Be hospitable to one another without grumbling. As each has received a gift, employ it in serving one another, as good managers of the grace of God in its various forms. (1 Peter 4:8–10 WEB)

In Revelation, Jesus addressed the main seven churches at that time, but during this church era, the Millennial, Jesus is addressing all the churches. There are many Christian religions around the world today, and Christ will address them all to repent their sins, give warnings and commendations, plus a promise to overcomers. Remember that we are one body of Christ through our own church; many parts, but one body.

> For even as we have many members in one body, and all the members don't have the same function. (Romans 12:4 WEB)

Jesus esteems us in our church, and we are held in great respect and admiration for being a part of it. There are seven commands that Jesus gives us, and a church is where these commands are fulfilled: Be baptized and make others disciples.

> Go and make disciples of all nations, baptizing them in the name of the Father and of the Son and of the Holy Spirit. (Matthew 28:19 WEB)

Repent and believe.

> "The time is fulfilled, and God's Kingdom is at hand! Repent, and believe in the Good News." (Mark 1:15 WEB)

To Love.

> Jesus said to him, "'You shall love the Lord your God with all your heart, with all your soul, and with all your mind.' This is the first and great

commandment. A second likewise is this, 'You shall love your neighbor as yourself.'" (Matthew 22:37–39 WEB)

Jesus taught us how to pray.
Pray like this:

"'Our Father in heaven, may your name be kept holy. Let your Kingdom come. Let your will be done on earth as it is in heaven. Give us today our daily bread. Forgive us our debts, as we also forgive our debtors. Bring us not into temptation but deliver us from the evil one. For yours is the Kingdom, the power, and the glory forever. Amen.'" (Matthew 6:9–13 WEB)

Attend the Lord's supper. During Catholic mass, the holy Eucharist and wine that is offered is the body and blood of Jesus.

He took bread, and when he had given thanks, he broke, and gave it to them, saying, "This is my body which is given for you. Do this in memory of me." Likewise, he took the cup after supper, saying, "This cup is the new covenant in my blood, which is poured out for you." (Luke 22:19–20 WEB)

To give to those in need.

"Give, and it will be given to you: good measure, pressed down, shaken together, and running over, will be given to you. For with the same measure you measure it will be measured back to you." (Luke 6:38 WEB)

Sister Regina said that the church was not a house built for saints, but a hospital built for sinners. So let's all go to church and seek reconciliation; after all, we are only human, and we know that humans are sinful by nature. Remember the Sabbath Day, and keep it holy. Going to church every Sunday will help us remember the teachings of Jesus so that we can live a life for Christ and not a self-indulgent one. Jesus looks forward to seeing you in mass and worshiping the One True God.

> For it is written, "'As I live,' says the Lord, 'to me every knee will bow. Every tongue will confess to God.'" (Romans 14:11 WEB)

May the Grace of God be with you all. Amen.

THE DEPTHS OF CHASM

A chasm is a deep fissure in the earth, rock, or another surface and a gulf or breach. It is also a profound difference and division or separation between people and their viewpoints and feelings. For instance, Jesus is always talking about the chasm between the rich and poor, the clothed and naked, the fed and hungry, the healthy and sick, separating the sheep from the goats.

> And besides all this, between us and you a great chasm has been set in place, so that those who want to go from here to you cannot, nor can anyone cross over from there to us. (Luke 16:26 NIV)

Jesus also asks that we shrink that distance between our profound differences with people.

> Now I beg you, brothers, through the name of our Lord, Jesus Christ, that you all speak the same thing, and that there be no divisions among you, but that you be perfected together

in the same mind and in the same judgment. (1 Corinthians 1:10 WEB)

Here Jesus describes what will happen to those who did or did not make a difference during their lifetime. This is the price a person pays when the depths of chasm are ignored.

"When the Son of Man comes in his glory, and all the angels with him, he will sit on his glorious throne. All the nations will be gathered before him, and he will separate the people one from another as a shepherd separates the sheep from the goats. He will put the sheep on his right and the goats on his left.

"Then the King will say to those on his right, 'Come, you who are blessed by my Father; take your inheritance, the kingdom prepared for you since the creation of the world. For I was hungry and you gave me something to eat, I was thirsty and you gave me something to drink, I was a stranger and you invited me in, I needed clothes and you clothed me, I was sick and you looked after me, I was in prison and you came to visit me.'

"Then the righteous will answer him, 'Lord, when did we see you hungry and feed you, or thirsty and give you something to drink? When did we see you a stranger and invite you in, or needing clothes and clothe you? When did we see you sick or in prison and go to visit you?' "The King will reply, 'Truly I tell you, whatever you did for one of the least of these brothers and sisters of mine, you did for me.'

"Then he will say to those on his left, 'Depart from me, you who are cursed, into the eternal fire prepared for the devil and his angels.

For I was hungry and you gave me nothing to eat,
I was thirsty and you gave me nothing to drink,
I was a stranger and you did not invite me in, I
needed clothes and you did not clothe me, I was
sick and in prison and you did not look after me.'

"They also will answer, 'Lord, when did we
see you hungry or thirsty or a stranger or needing clothes or sick or in prison, and did not help
you?'

"He will reply, 'Truly I tell you, whatever
you did not do for one of the least of these, you
did not do for me.'

"Then they will go away to eternal punishment, but the righteous to eternal life." (Matthew
25:31–46 NIV)

Through Christ's teachings, we learn to have a change of heart
toward people and live a life helping others. We learn to not be
obsessed with possessions and to really care about others' needs spiritually and physically. This is called *metanoia*, a change in one's way
of life resulting from penitence or spiritual conversion—a complete
change of heart.

A person who is luxuriously self-indulgent and lives in an
extravagant way has fallen into a state of moral decay. Jesus says that
living a decadent life can cause a decline in society. We must listen
to Christ and learn to live a life of loving others. Christ teaches us to
use self-control on our behavior toward others and have compassion
for people and their feelings. We need Christ's constant companion-
ship, spiritual guidance, and penitence. Practice daily the teachings
of Jesus, and learn to live a life for Christ and not a self-indulgent one
before it's too late. Sister Regina, my spiritual director, said that it is
like the parable of Lazarus and the rich man.

"Now there was a certain rich man, and
he was clothed in purple and fine linen, living
in luxury every day. A certain beggar, named

Lazarus, was taken to his gate, full of sores, and desiring to be fed with the crumbs that fell from the rich man's table. Yes, even the dogs came and licked his sores. The beggar died, and he was carried away by the angels to Abraham's bosom. The rich man also died and was buried. In Hades, he lifted up his eyes, being in torment, and saw Abraham far off, and Lazarus at his bosom. He cried and said, 'Father Abraham, have mercy on me, and send Lazarus, that he may dip the tip of his finger in water, and cool my tongue! For I am in anguish in this flame.'

"But Abraham said, 'Son, remember that you, in your lifetime, received your good things, and Lazarus, in the same way, bad things. But here he is now comforted, and you are in anguish. Besides all this, between us and you there is a great gulf fixed, that those who want to pass from here to you are not able, and that no one may cross over from there to us.'

"He said, 'I ask you therefore, father, that you would send him to my father's house; for I have five brothers, that he may testify to them, so they won't also come into this place of torment.'

"But Abraham said to him, 'They have Moses and the prophets. Let them listen to them.'

"He said, 'No, father Abraham, but if one goes to them from the dead, they will repent.'

"He said to him, 'If they don't listen to Moses and the prophets, neither will they be persuaded if one rises from the dead.'" (Luke 16:19–31 WEB)

The Lord helps us to see the truth and understand the importance of shrinking the gap between boundaries and people in this world. He gives us eyes to see and ears to hear and a heart to understand. God desires for us to uncover His mercy with a continual cycle of healing. There are many charities, missionaries, the salvation army, food banks, and places for the homeless to go. Some cities are improving the schools to help raise the education for the citizens in the so-called lower-class areas. There are hospitals that will reduce the cost of service for those who can't afford insurance. Some countries don't have hot and cold running water in their homes, or electricity and gasoline. Members that live in tribal communities or in third-world countries don't have these luxuries but appreciate the missionaries that come and build small homes for them, feed them, and teach them about God.

Metanoia, or having a change of heart, is when a person goes from living a life of me, myself, and I to the Father, Son, and Holy Spirit. Just take a good look around, and you will see many businesses making a difference to shorten the depths of chasm. Where is your heart telling you to go and help make that difference?

GOD'S MOVABLE THRONE

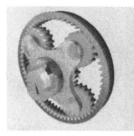  

God's movable throne is described here by a vision from Ezekiel and John. These scenes implicate a theocentric or God-centered universe, or just the fact that God's heavenly throne is the center of worship. Every element and creature are in direct relationship to the throne and God. The rainbow refers to God's promise to never destroy mankind, and the throne itself is laced in jasper and sardius-colored stones which represent the blood of our slain Christ who saved us from death. The visions of the wheels on the throne are identical to a mechanical mechanism called planetary gears or epicyclic gearing. Interestingly, this same system also refers to our planetary orbital paths in the heavens. It would be very hard to describe a vision of gears to a machine not yet built for another two to eight thousand years later. We commonly use these gears today, but in biblical times, they did not have machines like tractors, industrial automation machines, robotics, or even cars. For all we know, God may come down in a Harrier Jump Jet.

> The appearance of the wheels and their work was like a beryl. The four of them had one likeness. Their appearance and their work was as it were a wheel within a wheel. When they went, they went in their four directions. They didn't turn when they went. As for their rims, they were high and dreadful; and the four of them had their rims full of eyes all around.

When the living creatures went, the wheels went beside them. When the living creatures were lifted up from the earth, the wheels were lifted up. Wherever the spirit was to go, they went. The spirit was to go there. The wheels were lifted up beside them; for the spirit of the living creature was in the wheels. When those went, these went. When those stood, these stood. When those were lifted up from the earth, the wheels were lifted up beside them; for the spirit of the living creature was in the wheels. (Ezekiel 1:16–21 WEB)

Immediately I was in the Spirit. Behold, there was a throne set in heaven, and one sitting on the throne that looked like a jasper stone and a sardius. There was a rainbow around the throne, like an emerald to look at. Before the throne was something like a sea of glass, similar to crystal. In the middle of the throne, and around the throne were four living creatures full of eyes before and behind. The first creature was like a lion, and the second creature like a calf, and the third creature had a face like a man, and the fourth was like a flying eagle. The four living creatures, each one of them having six wings, are full of eyes around and within. They have no rest day and night, saying, "Holy, holy, holy is the Lord God, the Almighty, who was and who is and who is to come!"

When the living creatures give glory, honor, and thanks to him who sits on the throne, to him who lives forever and ever. (Revelation 4:2–9 WEB)

Then Moses, Aaron, Nadab, Abihu, and seventy of the elders of Israel went up. They saw the God of Israel. Under his feet was like a paved work of sapphire stone, like the skies for clearness. He didn't lay his hand on the nobles of the children of Israel. They saw God and ate and drank. (Exodus 24:9–11 WEB)

All things radiate and flow from God's throne: His creation and human history. God's sovereignty over all things is represented by the throne and to Him whom this world solely belongs to.

HOLLOW SHELL

I would like to use this sunflower in reference to the final judgment when Christ returns in all His glory and pronounces the final word on all of history. What will He find in you?

This sunflower was thirteen feet tall and grew to be seventeen inches wide. It was very impressive in size and full of seeds. At harvest time, I was surprised to find that the shells were hollow. Only a very few had seeds inside. The Bible tells us that we are to produce much fruit in our lifetime.

> that you may walk worthily of the Lord, to please him in all respects, bearing fruit in every good work and increasing in the knowledge of God. (Colossians 1:10 WEB)

Bearing fruit is to nurture, encouraging growth and development to others, sharing in the knowledge of God, and being disciples for Jesus. Doing good works for others by using the talented gift given to you by the Holy Spirit—preaching, teaching, serving, writing, firefighting, healing, giving, etc. There are all kinds of tools that God gives people to help others. It's God's way of helping the suffering in this world.

"In this my Father is glorified, that you bear much fruit; and so you will be my disciples." (John 15:8 WEB)

But some people just do it halfway; their actions only make them look good and impressive on the outside but keep the false secrets hidden inside like a hollow shell. They don't have enough time to go to church or to help the poor or to feed the hungry or to just love people for who they are, like Jesus did. They really don't care all that much about Jesus and what He did for us. During the crucifixion and death, Jesus completely humiliated Himself for our salvation, and those that don't really care to give their expression of thanks to God are, in actuality, humiliating Jesus! So it is fitting that God appoints Jesus to be our final judge.

When you are standing in front of Jesus to be judged, will He find your actions exalting Jesus suitable for recompense, or will He find that your actions in life was one of a humiliating hollow shell?

When you grab all you can get, that's what happens: the more you get, the less you are. (Proverbs 1:19–29 MSG)

Even now the ax lies at the root of the trees. Therefore every tree that doesn't produce good fruit is cut down, and cast into the fire. (Matthew 3:10 WEB)

I pray that Jesus will find faith inside all of us.

Therefore produce fruit worthy of repentance! (Matthew 3:8 WEB)

Amen.

THE SCROLL AND THE LAMB

The seven-sealed scroll is an ancient document signifying fullness and completeness.

> When I looked, behold, a hand was stretched out to me; and, behold, a scroll of a book was in it. He spread it before me. It was written within and without; and lamentations, mourning, and woe were written in it. (Ezekiel 2:9–10 WEB)

Jesus Christ is the only one worthy to open it, and as the contents are unfolded, it is the blessings of the covenant promise of life from God to those who worship Christ and the curse of death that falls on the disobedient. God's plans for the redemption of His world.

> I saw, in the right hand of him who sat on the throne, a book written inside and outside, sealed shut with seven seals. I saw a mighty angel proclaiming with a loud voice, "Who is worthy to open the book, and to break its seals?" No one in heaven above, or on the earth, or under the earth, was able to open the book or to look in it. Then I wept much, because no one was found worthy to open the book or to look in it. One of the elders said to me, "Don't weep. Behold, the Lion who is of the tribe of Judah, the Root of David, has overcome: he who opens the book and its seven seals." I saw in the middle of the throne and of

the four living creatures, and in the middle of the elders, a Lamb standing, as though it had been slain, having seven horns and seven eyes, which are the seven Spirits of God, sent out into all the earth. Then he came, and he took it out of the right hand of him who sat on the throne. Now when he had taken the book, the four living creatures and the twenty-four elders fell down before the Lamb, each one having a harp, and golden bowls full of incense, which are the prayers of the saints. They sang a new song, saying,

"You are worthy to take the book
and to open its seals:
for you were killed,
and bought us for God with your blood
out of every tribe, language, people, and nation,
and made us kings and priests to our God,
and we will reign on the earth."

I saw, and I heard something like a voice of many angels around the throne, the living creatures, and the elders. The number of them was ten thousands of ten thousands, and thousands of thousands; saying with a loud voice, "Worthy is the Lamb who has been killed to receive the power, wealth, wisdom, strength, honor, glory, and blessing!"

I heard every created thing which is in heaven, on the earth, under the earth, on the sea, and everything in them, saying, "To him who sits on the throne, and to the Lamb be the blessing, the honor, the glory, and the dominion, forever and ever! Amen.

The four living creatures said, "Amen!" Then the elders fell down and worshiped (Revelation 5:1–14 WEB)

THE FOUR HORSEMEN
OF THE APOCALYPSE

The description ordering judgment to the world is told in three sets of seven events in different ways: the seven seals, the seven trumpets, and the seven bowls. This is a recapitulation of history, the same events revealed and retold. Jesus describes the judgment in terms of war, international conflict, famine, pestilence, persecution, earthquakes, and the destruction of God's creation. Over time, all these events replay over and over again throughout the course of history. The real question is, when are we going to learn from our mistakes? Believers of Christ see the suffering of the world today as tribulation. The Hebrew word for tribulation is *tsara*, which means "narrow, compressed, distress or affliction."

The rider on the red horse represents war and international conflict, nations rising against nations, and man fighting against each other. He brings a time of bloodshed, assassinations, revolutions, murders, and riots. It is sad to see how people treat each other today! It must make God cry at our violent behavior.

The rider on the black horse represents famine, hunger, and starvation. There has always been world hunger, people who don't have money or the proper means to feed their family; but even now with COVID-19, the wealthy or upper class are unable to just buy groceries at the stores because the shelves are empty.

The rider on the white horse represents the Antichrist who will convince everyone that he brings peace in the midst of global turmoil. Well, he may bring peace to the middle east, but don't believe his false promises because he is a wolf in sheep's clothing. He will be by far the worst tyrant to ever appear on earth!

The rider on the pale horse represents pestilence, plagues that bring death to people all over the world. We have had terrible nightmare bacteria and diseases over the years, but this COVID-19 pandemic is a war. This virus has spread worldwide, causing an outbreak of fear and an economic crisis!

The four horsemen are angels of the Lord. In the Old Testament, the prophet Zechariah asked the Lord who they were.

> Again, I lifted up my eyes, and saw, and behold, four chariots came out from between two mountains; and the mountains were mountains of bronze. In the first chariot were red horses; in the second chariot black horses; in the third chariot white horses; and in the fourth chariot dappled horses, all of them powerful. Then I asked the angel who talked with me, "What are these, my lord?"
>
> The angel answered me, "These are the four winds of the sky, which go out from standing before the Lord of all the earth. The one with the black horses goes out toward the north country; and the white went out after them; and the dappled went out toward the south country." The strong went out and sought to go that they might walk back and forth through the earth: and he said, "Go around and through the earth!" So, they walked back and forth through the earth. (Zechariah 6:1–7 WEB)

In Revelation, the four horsemen begin their quest:

> I saw that the Lamb opened one of the seven seals, and I heard one of the four living creatures saying, as with a voice of thunder, "Come and

see!" Then a white horse appeared, and he who sat on it had a bow. A crown was given to him, and he came out conquering, and to conquer.

When he opened the second seal, I heard the second living creature saying, "Come!" Another came out: a red horse. To him who sat on it was given power to take peace from the earth, and that they should kill one another. There was given to him a great sword.

When he opened the third seal, I heard the third living creature saying, "Come and see!" And behold, a black horse, and he who sat on it had a balance in his hand. I heard a voice in the middle of the four living creatures saying, "A choenix of wheat for a denarius, and three choenix of barley for a denarius! Don't damage the oil and the wine!"

When he opened the fourth seal, I heard the fourth living creature saying, "Come and see!" And behold, a pale horse, and the name of he who sat on it was Death. Hades followed with him. Authority over one fourth of the earth, to kill with the sword, with famine, with death, and by the wild animals of the earth was given to him.

When he opened the fifth seal, I saw underneath the altar the souls of those who had been killed for the Word of God, and for the testimony of the Lamb which they had. They cried with a loud voice, saying, "How long, Master, the holy and true, until you judge and avenge our blood on those who dwell on the earth?" A long white robe was given to each of them. They were told that they should rest yet for a while, until their fellow servants and their brothers, who would also be killed even as they were, should complete their course.

I saw when he opened the sixth seal, and there was a great earthquake. The sun became black as sackcloth made of hair, and the whole moon became as blood. The stars of the sky fell to the earth, like a fig tree dropping its unripe figs when it is shaken by a great wind. The sky was removed like a scroll when it is rolled up. Every mountain and island was moved out of its place. The kings of the earth, the princes, the commanding officers, the rich, the strong, and every slave and free person, hid themselves in the caves and in the rocks of the mountains. They told the mountains and the rocks, "Fall on us, and hide us from the face of him who sits on the throne, and from the wrath of the Lamb, for the great day of his wrath has come; and who is able to stand?" (Revelation 6:1–17 WEB)

In chapter 7, the seals describe who are able to stand the wrath of God:

I saw another angel ascend from the sunrise, having the seal of the living God. He cried with a loud voice to the four angels to whom it was given to harm the earth and the sea, saying, "Don't harm the earth, the sea, or the trees, until we have sealed the bondservants of our God on their foreheads!" …After these things I looked, and behold, a great multitude, which no man could count, out of every nation and of all tribes, peoples, and languages, standing before the throne and before the Lamb, dressed in white robes, with palm branches in their hands. They cried with a loud voice, saying, "Salvation be to our God, who sits on the throne, and to the Lamb!" (Revelation 7:2–3; 9–10 WEB)

Jesus promises that His Father will take care of the ones who come out of tribulation:

> He said to me, "These are those who came out of the great suffering. They washed their robes, and made them white in the Lamb's blood. Therefore they are before the throne of God, they serve him day and night in his temple. He who sits on the throne will spread his tabernacle over them. They will never be hungry or thirsty any more. The sun won't beat on them, nor any heat; for the Lamb who is in the middle of the throne shepherds them and leads them to springs of life-giving waters. And God will wipe away every tear from their eyes. (Revelation 7:14–17 WEB)

In chapters 8 and 9 describe the seven trumpets and seven bowls. The angels with trumpets make loud noises upon the Earth, and death and destruction follow. The seven bowls are plagues set upon man:

> I saw the seven angels who stand before God, and seven trumpets were given to them… The angel took the censer, and he filled it with the fire of the altar, then threw it on the earth. Thunders, sounds, lightnings, and an earthquake followed. (Revelation 8:2, 5 WEB)

> They were given power, not to kill them, but to torment them for five months. Their torment was like the torment of a scorpion when it strikes a person. In those days people will seek death, and will in no way find it. They will desire to die, and death will flee from them. (Revelation 9:5–6 WEB)

These next gospel passages point to the destruction of Jerusalem and foreshadow God's judgment at the end of times. Jesus says to keep watch and know what the signs are, be prepared to drop everything and go when the time has come, love and help your neighbors, and most of all, do not be afraid.

Jesus went out from the temple and was going on his way. His disciples came to him to show him the buildings of the temple. But he answered them, "You see all of these things, don't you? Most certainly I tell you, there will not be left here one stone on another, that will not be thrown down."

As he sat on the Mount of Olives, the disciples came to him privately, saying, "Tell us, when will these things be? What is the sign of your coming, and of the end of the age?"

Jesus answered them, "Be careful that no one leads you astray. For many will come in my name, saying, 'I am the Christ,' and will lead many astray. You will hear of wars and rumors of wars. See that you aren't troubled, for all this must happen, but the end is not yet. For nation will rise against nation, and kingdom against kingdom; and there will be famines, plagues, and earthquakes in various places. But all these things are the beginning of birth pains.

"Then they will deliver you up to oppression and will kill you. You will be hated by all of the nations for my name's sake. Then many will stumble, and will deliver up one another, and will hate one another. Many false prophets will arise and will lead many astray. Because iniquity will be multiplied, the love of many will grow cold. But he who endures to the end will be saved. This Good News of the Kingdom will be preached in the whole world for a testimony to all the nations, and then the end will come." (Matthew 24:1–14 WEB)

As he went out of the temple, one of his disciples said to him, "Teacher, see what kind of stones and what kind of buildings!"

Jesus said to him, "Do you see these great buildings? There will not be left here one stone on another, which will not be thrown down."

As he sat on the Mount of Olives opposite the temple, Peter, James, John, and Andrew asked him privately, "Tell us, when will these things be? What is the sign that these things are all about to be fulfilled?"

Jesus, answering, began to tell them, "Be careful that no one leads you astray. For many will come in my name, saying, 'I am he!' and will lead many astray.

"When you hear of wars and rumors of wars, don't be troubled. For those must happen, but the end is not yet. For nation will rise against nation, and kingdom against kingdom. There will be earthquakes in various places. There will be famines and troubles. These things are the beginning of birth pains. But watch yourselves, for they will deliver you up to councils. You will be beaten in synagogues. You will stand before rulers and kings for my sake, for a testimony to them. The Good News must first be preached to all the nations. When they lead you away and deliver you up, don't be anxious beforehand, or premeditate what you will say, but say whatever will be given you in that hour. For it is not you who speak, but the Holy Spirit.

"Brother will deliver up brother to death, and the father his child. Children will rise up against parents, and cause them to be put to death. You will be hated by all men for my name's sake, but he who endures to the end will be saved. But when you see the abomination of desolation, spoken of by Daniel the prophet, standing where it ought not" (let the reader understand), "then let those who are in Judea flee to the mountains, and let him who is on the housetop not go down, nor enter in, to take anything out of his house. Let him who is in the field not return back to take his cloak. But woe to those who are with child and to those who nurse babies in those days! Pray that your flight won't be in the winter. For in those days there will be oppression, such as there has not been the like from the beginning of the creation which God created until now, and never will be. Unless the Lord had shortened the days, no flesh would have been saved; but for the sake of the chosen ones, whom he picked out, he shortened the days. Then if anyone tells you, 'Look, here is the Christ!' or, 'Look, there!' don't believe it. For there will arise false christs and false prophets, and will show signs and wonders, that they may lead astray, if possible, even the chosen ones. But you watch.

"Behold, I have told you all things before-hand. But in those days, after that oppression, the sun will be darkened, the moon will not give its light, the stars will be falling from the sky, and the powers that are in the heavens will be shaken. Then they will see the Son of Man coming in clouds with great power and glory. Then he will send out his angels and will gather together his chosen ones from the four winds, from the ends of the earth to the ends of the sky.

"Now from the fig tree, learn this parable. When the branch has now become tender, and produces its leaves, you know that the summer is near; even so you also, when you see these things coming to pass, know that it is near, at the doors. Most certainly I say to you, this generation will not pass away until all these things happen. Heaven and earth will pass away, but my words will not pass away. But of that day or that hour no one knows, not even the angels in heaven, nor the Son, but only the Father. Watch, keep alert, and pray; for you don't know when the time is.

"It is like a man, traveling to another country, having left his house, and given authority to his servants, and to each one his work, and also commanded the doorkeeper to keep watch. Watch therefore, for you don't know when the lord of the house is coming, whether at evening, or at midnight, or when the rooster crows, or in the morning; lest coming suddenly he might find you sleeping. What I tell you, I tell all: Watch." (Mark 13:1–37 WEB) (See reference: Daniel 9:17; 11:31; 12:11; Isaiah 13:10; 34:4)

He said, "Watch out that you don't get led astray, for many will come in my name, saying, 'I am he,' and, 'The time is at hand.' Therefore, don't follow them. When you hear of wars and disturbances, don't be terrified, for these things must happen first, but the end won't come immediately."

Then he said to them, "Nation will rise against nation, and kingdom against kingdom. There will be great earthquakes, famines, and plagues in various places. There will be terrors and great signs from heaven. But before all these things, they will lay their hands on you and will persecute you, delivering you up to synagogues and prisons, bringing you before kings and governors for my name's sake. It will turn out as a testimony for you. Settle it therefore in your hearts not to meditate beforehand how to answer, for I will give you a mouth and wisdom which all your adversaries will not be able to withstand or to contradict. You will be handed over even by parents, brothers, relatives, and friends. They will cause some of you to be put to death. You will be hated by all men for my name's sake. And not a hair of your head will perish.

"By your endurance you will win your lives.

"But when you see Jerusalem surrounded by armies, then know that its desolation is at hand. Then let those who are in Judea flee to the mountains. Let those who are in the middle of her depart. Let those who are in the country not enter therein. For these are days of vengeance, that all things which are written may be fulfilled. Woe to those who are pregnant and to those who nurse infants in those days! For there will be great distress in the land, and wrath to this people. They will fall by the edge of the sword and will be led captive into all the nations. Jerusalem will be trampled down by the Gentiles, until the times of the Gentiles are fulfilled. There will be signs in the sun, moon, and stars; and on the earth anxiety of nations, in perplexity for the roaring of the sea and the waves; men fainting for fear, and for expectation of the things which are coming on the world: for the powers of the heavens will be shaken. Then they will see the Son of Man coming in a cloud with power and great glory. But when these things begin to happen, look up and lift up your heads, because your redemption is near."

He told them a parable. "See the fig tree and all the trees. When they are already budding, you see it and know by your own selves that the summer is already near. Even so you also, when you see these things happening, know that God's Kingdom is near. Most certainly I tell you, this generation will not pass away until all things are accomplished. Heaven and earth will pass away, but my words will by no means pass away.

"So be careful, or your hearts will be loaded down with carousing, drunkenness, and cares of this life, and that day will come on you suddenly. For it will come like a snare on all those who dwell on the surface of all the earth. Therefore, be watchful all the time, praying that you may be counted worthy to escape all these things that will happen, and to stand before the Son of Man." (Luke 21:8–36 WEB)

With all these facts before us, how do we respond during times of trouble? It will be a time for us to focus on our faith and not the crisis or the panic. Tribulation is a reality; the Bible speaks only truth. In these kinds of situations, Jesus tells us to not be fearful but faithful. Strong faith will bring forth peace, love, and unity in the kingdom of Christ.

THE ANTICHRIST

The Antichrist will be a person of great power and, through Satan, can use this power to swallow up whole nations. He will fully know how to manipulate and control people.

> He shall come in peaceably and seize the kingdom by intrigue. (Daniel 11:21 NKJV)

He will arrive on the political scene in a nonconductive way and not necessarily of any denomination. He will gain favor by intriguing common ordinary people but with a complex entanglement in mind.

Satan has inspired world leaders for centuries, but in the final days, Satan and the Antichrist will be defeated.

> For many deceivers have gone out into the world, those who don't confess that Jesus Christ came in the flesh. This is the deceiver and the Antichrist. (2 John 1:7 WEB)

Anti means "instead of." He will oppose Christ and say that he is, himself, the Christ.

And it performed great signs, even causing fire to come down from heaven to the earth in full view of the people. (Revelation 13:13, NIV)

Let no one deceive you in any way. For it will not be, unless the rebellion comes first, and the man of sin is revealed, the son of destruction, he who opposes and exalts himself against all that is called God or that is worshiped, so that he sits as God in the temple of God, setting himself up as God. (2 Thessalonians 2:3–4 WEB)

Once the Antichrist has control, he will create havoc and chaos and demand that everyone bows to him and only him, or be tortured. His followers must wear his mark on their forehead, "666."

Here is wisdom. Let him who has understanding calculate the number of the beast, for it is the number of a man: His number *is* 666. (Revelation 13:18 NKJV)

He will be more despicable and fiercer than the German politician Adolf Hitler, the leader of the Nazi Party; or the Soviet politician Joseph Stalin, known as the Man of Steel; and even the Chinese communist Mao Zedong ever were.

The Bible doesn't tell exactly when that will be but that we should be aware of his coming before Armageddon.

Little children, these are the end times, and as you heard that the Antichrist is coming, even now many antichrists have arisen. By this we know that it is the final hour. They went out from us, but they didn't belong to us; for if they had belonged to us, they would have continued with us. But they left, that they might be revealed that none of them belong to us. You have an anointing from the Holy One, and you all have knowledge. I have not written to you because you don't know the truth, but because you know it, and because no lie is of the truth. Who is the liar but he who denies that Jesus is the Christ? This is the Antichrist, he who denies the Father and the Son. (1 John 2:18–22 WEB)

and every spirit who doesn't confess that Jesus Christ has come in the flesh is not of God, and this is the spirit of the Antichrist, of whom you have heard that it comes. Now it is in the world already. (1 John 4:3 WEB)

At this point in time, all Christians should be bowing to God to please release them of this nightmare during the reign of the Antichrist. Us Christians will have Christ's name written on our forehead! The Antichrist will know exactly who to target first!

At the same time, we must not forget that the Antichrist is just a human with limited powers and is not God! God is the one with absolute control over all things; this is only the final test and battle between good and evil. When it is all over, no enemy of God's will be allowed to cross the boundary into eternal life; they will be destroyed by the breath of Jesus. Only God's people will be allowed to enter the new kingdom into eternal life and into heaven for all eternity.

And then the lawless one will be revealed, whom the Lord Jesus will overthrow with the breath of his mouth and destroy by the splendor of his coming. (2 Thessalonians 2:8 NIV)

May the peace of the Lord be with you always. Amen.

ARMAGEDDON

Armageddon is the final battle between good and evil on earth, where Christ and His army defeat Satan, the Antichrist, and their followers. In chapters 11 through 16 is where the cosmic stage of this battle is set. Mother Mary and her child, who is to rule the nations, are attacked by the devil. He comes as a dragon and a false prophet to deceive mankind. The outcome will be the fulfillment of God's throne on Earth, and the kingdom of Christ will be established for all eternity.

A great sign was seen in heaven: a woman clothed with the sun, and the moon under her feet, and on her head a crown of twelve stars. She was with child. She cried out in pain, laboring to give birth. Another sign was seen in heaven. Behold, a great red dragon, having seven heads and ten horns, and on his heads seven crowns. His tail drew one third of the stars of the sky and threw them to the earth. The dragon stood before the woman who was about to give birth, so that when she gave birth, he might devour her child. She gave birth to a son, a male child, who is to rule all the nations with a rod of iron. Her child was caught up to God, and to his throne. The woman fled into the wilderness, where she has a place prepared by God, that there they may nourish her one thousand two hundred sixty days.

There was war in the sky. Michael and his angels made war on the dragon. The dragon and his angels made war. They didn't prevail. No place was found for them any more in heaven. The great dragon was thrown down, the old serpent, he who is called the devil and Satan, the deceiver of the whole world. He was thrown down to the earth, and his angels were thrown down with him. I heard a loud voice in heaven, saying, "Now the salvation, the power, and the Kingdom of our God, and the authority of his Christ has come; for the accuser of our brothers has been thrown down, who accuses them before our God day and night. They overcame him because of the Lamb's blood, and because of the word of their testimony. They didn't love their life, even to death. Therefore rejoice, heavens, and you who dwell in them. Woe to the earth and to the sea, because the devil has gone down to you, having great wrath, knowing that he has but a short time." (Revelation 12:1–12 WEB)

I saw another beast coming up out of the earth. He had two horns like a lamb, and he spoke like a dragon. He exercises all the authority of the first beast in his presence. He makes the earth and those who dwell in it to worship the first beast, whose fatal wound was healed. He performs great signs, even making fire come down out of the sky to the earth in the sight of people. He deceives my own people who dwell on the earth because of the signs he was granted to do in front of the beast, saying to those who dwell on the earth that they should make an image to the beast who had the sword wound and lived. It was given to him to give breath to it, to the image of the beast, that the image of the beast should both speak, and cause as many as wouldn't worship the image of the beast to be killed. He causes all, the small and the great, the rich and the poor, and the free and the slave, to be given marks on their right hands, or on their foreheads; and that no one would be able to buy or to sell, unless he has that mark, which is the name of the beast or the number of his name. Here is wisdom. He who has understanding, let him calculate the number of the beast, for it is the number of a man. His number is six hundred sixty-six. (Revelation 13:11–18 WEB)

The Defeat of Satan and the Kingdom of Christ

I saw, and behold, the Lamb standing on Mount Zion, and with him a number, one hundred forty-four thousand, having his name, and the name of his Father, written on their foreheads. I heard a sound from heaven, like the sound of many waters, and like the sound of a great thunder. The sound which I heard was like that of harpists playing on their harps. They sing a new song before the throne, and before the four living creatures and the elders. No one could learn the song except the one hundred forty-four thousand, those who had been redeemed out of the earth. These are those who were not defiled with women, for they are virgins. These are those who follow the Lamb wherever he goes. These were redeemed by Jesus from among men, the first fruits to God and to the Lamb. In their mouth was found no lie, for they are blameless. (Revelation 14:1–5 WEB)

I looked, and saw a white cloud, and on the cloud one sitting like a son of man, having on his head a golden crown, and in his hand a sharp sickle. Another angel came out of the temple, crying with a loud voice to him who sat on the cloud, "Send your sickle, and reap; for the hour to reap has come; for the harvest of the earth is ripe!" He who sat on the cloud thrust his sickle on the earth, and the earth was reaped. (Revelation 14:14–16 WEB) (See reference: Daniel 7:13)

I saw another great and marvelous sign in the sky: seven angels having the seven last plagues, for in them God's wrath is finished. (Revelation 15:1 WEB)

I saw coming out of the mouth of the dragon, and out of the mouth of the beast, and out of the mouth of the false prophet, three unclean spirits, something like frogs; for they are spirits of demons, performing signs; which go out to the kings of the whole inhabited earth, to gather them together for the war of that great day of God, the Almighty.

"Behold, I come like a thief. Blessed is he who watches, and keeps his clothes, so that he doesn't walk naked, and they see his shame." He gathered them together into the place which is called in Hebrew, "Megiddo".

The seventh poured out his bowl into the air. A loud voice came out of the temple of heaven, from the throne, saying, "It is done!" (Revelation 16:13–17 WEB)

The word *Megiddo* in Hebrew comes from the term *har megiddo*, which means "mount or hill of Megiddo." In the KJV Bible, the scripture reads: "He gathered them together into a place called in the Hebrew tongue Armageddon" (Revelation 16:16 KJV).

The battle of Armageddon, or Megiddo, is prophesied to be taken place here because there have been hundreds of battles fought and won on this hill located about sixty miles north of Jerusalem. It will be a cataclysmic event where Christ comes on His white horse to triumph over the beast, the false prophet, Antichrist, Satan, and all their followers.

BABYLON HARLOT

The Babylon harlot is the alluring woman sitting upon a beast who seduces the kings of the unrepentant world. This is when the final judgments of God are poured out upon the unbelieving world. During the rapture, God allowed Christians to escape the seven-year nightmare of tribulation:

> Because you kept my command to endure, I also will keep you from the hour of testing which is to come on the whole world, to test those who dwell on the earth. (Revelation 3:10 WEB)

But after the battle between good and evil comes the final earthly judgments on the seven churches who witnessed the seven seals, the seven trumpets, and the seven bowls. Christ is now going to challenge these churches to be faithful to the end and receive their inheritance.

> One of the seven angels who had the seven bowls came and spoke with me, saying, "Come here. I will show you the judgment of the great prostitute who sits on many waters, with whom

the kings of the earth committed sexual immorality. Those who dwell in the earth were made drunken with the wine of her sexual immorality." He carried me away in the Spirit into a wilderness. I saw a woman sitting on a scarlet-colored beast, full of blasphemous names, having seven heads and ten horns. The woman was dressed in purple and scarlet, and decked with gold and precious stones and pearls, having in her hand a golden cup full of abominations and the impurities of the sexual immorality of the earth. And on her forehead a name was written, "MYSTERY, BABYLON THE GREAT, THE MOTHER OF THE PROSTITUTES AND OF THE ABOMINATIONS OF THE EARTH." I saw the woman drunken with the blood of the saints, and with the blood of the martyrs of Jesus. When I saw her, I wondered with great amazement? The angel said to me, "Why do you wonder? I will tell you the mystery of the woman, and of the beast that carries her, which has the seven heads and the ten horns. The beast that you saw was and is not; and is about to come up out of the abyss and to go into destruction. Those who dwell on the earth and whose names have not been written in the book of life from the foundation of the world will marvel when they see that the beast was, and is not, and shall be present. Here is the mind that has wisdom. The seven heads are seven mountains on which the woman sits. They are seven kings. Five have fallen, the one is, the other has not yet come. When he comes, he must continue a little while. The beast that was, and is not, is himself also an eighth, and is of the seven; and he goes to destruction. The ten horns that you saw are ten kings who have received no kingdom as yet, but they receive authority as kings with the beast for one hour. These have one mind, and they give their power and authority to the beast. These will war against the Lamb, and the Lamb will overcome them, for he is Lord of lords, and King of kings, and those who are with him are called chosen and faithful." He said to me, "The waters which you saw, where the prostitute sits, are peoples, multitudes, nations, and languages. The ten horns which you saw, and the beast, these will hate the prostitute, will make her desolate, will strip her naked, will eat her flesh, and will burn her utterly with fire. For God has put in their hearts to do what he has in mind, to be of one mind, and to give their kingdom to the beast, until the words of God should be accomplished. The woman whom you saw is the great city, which reigns over the kings of the earth." (Revelation 17:1–18 WEB)

The fruits which your soul lusted after have been lost to you. All things that were dainty and sumptuous have perished from you, and you will find them no more at all. The merchants of these things, who were made rich by her, will stand far away for the fear of her torment, weeping and mourning, saying, 'Woe, woe, the great city, she who was dressed in fine linen, purple, and scarlet, and decked with gold and precious stones and pearls! For in an hour such great riches are made desolate.' Every ship master, and everyone who sails anywhere, and mariners, and as many as gain their living by sea, stood far away, and cried out as they looked at the smoke of her burning, saying, 'What is like the great city?' They cast dust on their heads, and cried, weeping and mourning, saying, 'Woe, woe, the great city, in which all who had their ships in the sea were made rich by reason of her great wealth!' For she is made desolate in one hour.

"Rejoice over her, O heaven, you saints, apostles, and prophets; for God has judged your judgment on her." A mighty angel took up a stone like a great millstone and cast it into the sea, saying, "Thus with violence will Babylon, the great city, be thrown down, and will be found no more at all." (Revelation 18:14–21 WEB)

I saw the beast, and the kings of the earth, and their armies, gathered together to make war against him who sat on the horse, and against his army. The beast was taken, and with him the false prophet who worked the signs in his sight, with which he deceived those who had received the mark of the beast and those who worshiped his image. These two were thrown alive into the lake of fire that burns with sulfur. The rest were killed with the sword of him who sat on the horse, the sword which came out of his mouth. So all the birds were filled with their flesh. (Revelation 19:19–21 WEB)

Some people believe in universalism: the viewpoint that ultimately everyone will be saved, including those who reject God, reject the Bible, and even Satan will be brought together in cosmic harmony as a redeemed humanity. This notion of the essential divinity of every human being makes us partly god ourselves because we are essentially divine. The young people growing up today like this idea because no matter what they do, there are no consequences, and they will go to heaven. Unfortunately, this is not what the Bible tells us. Humans are sinful by nature and lost because of that, and so we are destined for hell. Only by the grace of God and the death and resurrection of Jesus that Christians will be saved and go to heaven.

> If anyone was not found written in the book of life, he was cast into the lake of fire. (Revelation 20:15 WEB)

The New Testament is very clear that only those who accept Jesus as their Lord and Savior will enter into the kingdom of heaven. Christians are coheirs of Jesus and will inherit what Jesus inherits from His Father.

> For you didn't receive the spirit of bondage again to fear, but you received the Spirit of adoption, by whom we cry, "Abba! Father!"
> The Spirit himself testifies with our spirit that we are children of God; and if children, then heirs: heirs of God and joint heirs with Christ, if indeed we suffer with him, that we may also be glorified with him. (Romans 8:15–17 WEB)

We are to be good stewards of this earth and pass on to generations, the highest Christian values of our Divine Lord Jesus Christ.

THOUSAND YEAR REIGN

This thousand-year reign that many talk about is thought to be the reign of Satan allowed to have control over people one last time, but it is actually God's chosen people who live and reign with Christ for a thousand years. Satan just has limited powers. This thousand-year reign is also called the Millennium, the Latin word *mille anni*, which we are living right now. There are many views on this point; some believe Christ comes before the tribulation, and others believe that Christ comes after the thousand years. Some believe that the whole "interadvent" period between the first and second comings of Christ is now in this church era.

Christ's reign began while He was here on earth and His kingdom was established with the growing of Christian churches. These churches house the visible signs of Jesus and offer a place of worship and sacred sacraments. They also are building Jesus's kingdom until He returns. No one really knows when Christ will return, but when He does, Satan will be restrained forever.

Biblical prophecies and promises must be fulfilled before Christ comes to establish His kingdom with justice and judgment. All the nations and people will gather together as one, including the resurrected dead, for the last judgment. Both the just and the unjust will come forth in the presence of Christ and be separated like sheep from the goats. The sheep will be resurrected into eternal life, and goats will be resurrected into eternal punishment. This judgment will reveal the truth about each person's relationship with God, especially those who suffered in life with broken and tattered wings. The consequences of the good works a person did or what they failed to do while living an earthly life. The righteous, humble, and meek will inherit the earth.

Blessed are the meek: for they shall inherit the earth. (Matthew 5:5 KJV)

The world is passing away with its lusts, but he who does God's will remains forever. (1 John 2:17 WEB)

But the humble shall inherit the land and shall delight themselves in the abundance of peace. (Psalm 37:11 WEB)

The angel said to her, "Don't be afraid, Mary, for you have found favor with God. Behold, you will conceive in your womb and give birth to a son and shall name him 'Jesus.' He will be great and will be called the Son of the Most High. The Lord God will give him the throne of his father David and he will reign over the house of Jacob forever. There will be no end to his Kingdom." (Luke 1:30–33 WEB)

Yes, all kings shall fall down before him. All nations shall serve him. (Psalm 72:11 WEB)

Of the increase of his government and of peace there shall be no end, on David's throne, and on his kingdom, to establish it, and to uphold it with justice and with righteousness from that time on, even forever. The zeal of Yahweh of Armies will perform this. (Isaiah 9:7 WEB)

> Then your people will all be righteous.
> They will inherit the land forever, the branch of
> my planting, the work of my hands, that I may
> be glorified. (Isaiah 60:21 WEB)

Despite the different views that people believe on the thousand-year reign, here is the scripture in revelation that gives the details of the judgment over good and evil and Satan being cast into the lake of fire:

> I saw an angel coming down out of heaven,
> having the key of the abyss and a great chain in
> his hand. He seized the dragon, the old serpent,
> which is the devil and Satan, who deceives the
> whole inhabited earth, and bound him for a
> thousand years, and cast him into the abyss, and
> shut it, and sealed it over him, that he should
> deceive the nations no more, until the thousand
> years were finished. After this, he must be freed
> for a short time. I saw thrones, and they sat on
> them, and judgment was given to them. I saw
> the souls of those who had been beheaded for the
> testimony of Jesus, and for the word of God, and
> such as didn't worship the beast nor his image,
> and didn't receive the mark on their forehead
> and on their hand. They lived and reigned with
> Christ for a thousand years. The rest of the dead
> didn't live until the thousand years were finished.
> This is the first resurrection. Blessed and holy is
> he who has part in the first resurrection. Over
> these, the second death has no power, but they
> will be priests of God and of Christ and will reign
> with him one thousand years.
> And after the thousand years, Satan will
> be released from his prison, and he will come
> out to deceive the nations which are in the four

corners of the earth, Gog and Magog, to gather them together to the war; the number of whom is as the sand of the sea. They went up over the width of the earth, and surrounded the camp of the saints, and the beloved city. Fire came down out of heaven from God and devoured them. The devil who deceived them was thrown into the lake of fire and sulfur, where the beast and the false prophet are also. They will be tormented day and night forever and ever.

I saw a great white throne, and him who sat on it, from whose face the earth and the heaven fled away. There was found no place for them. I saw the dead, the great and the small, standing before the throne, and they opened books. Another book was opened, which is the book of life. The dead were judged out of the things which were written in the books, according to their works. The sea gave up the dead who were in it. Death and Hades gave up the dead who were in them. They were judged, each one according to his works. Death and Hades were thrown into the lake of fire. This is the second death, the lake of fire. If anyone was not found written in the book of life, he was cast into the lake of fire. (Revelation 20 WEB)

CERBERUS

The Cerberus is a hell hound or the hound of Hades. It is a three-headed watchdog monster with a serpent's tail and lion's claws. In Greek Mythology, the Cerberus guards the gates of hell to prevent the dead from leaving the underworld. Some believe that if a living person tries to escape their death to hell, that he will go hunting for them. He also makes sure that the living is not permitted to visit Hades.

According to the myth there were three occasions where he was tricked: Heracles did with his strength, Orpheus with his music, and Sybil of Cumae with a honey cake. Another myth was when Psyche gave a barley cake to the Cerberus to be friendly to her so she could leave the underworld with Cupid. Psyche fell into a deep sleep, and Cupid escaped out the window and found her. Cupid lifted Psyche from the ground and carried her high into the heavens of Mount Olympus.

Only Jesus can waltz right past the Cerberus. This is what Jesus was referring to when He said that He has the keys to hell. After the crucifixion when Jesus died, He went to hell to gather the dead and bring them out, for only He will be the judge of the living and the dead.

He laid his right hand on me, saying, "Don't be afraid. I am the first and the last, and the Living one. I was dead, and behold, I am alive forever and ever. Amen. I have the keys of Death and of Hades." (Revelation 1:17–18 WEB)

The sea gave up the dead who were in it. Death and Hades gave up the dead who were in them. They were judged, each one according to his works. (Revelation 20:13 WEB)

The beast was taken, and with him the false prophet who worked the signs in his sight, with which he deceived those who had received the mark of the beast and those who worshiped his image. These two were thrown alive into the lake of fire that burns with sulfur. (Revelation 19:20 WEB)

THE MARRIAGE FEAST

Finally, heaven rejoices, for the Lord of lords has triumphed over the beast and false prophets. The bride of the Lamb is the faithful churches and their people. The marriage feast begins to celebrate with the final fulfillment of our Eucharist assemblies here on earth. Apostle Paul talks about this down payment that God gives us as a deposit for His children to inherit the earth. Then the glorious wedding comes!

In him you also, having heard the word of the truth, the Good News of your salvation—in whom, having also believed, you were sealed with the promised Holy Spirit, who is a pledge of our inheritance, to the redemption of God's own possession, to the praise of his glory.

For this cause I also, having heard of the faith in the Lord Jesus which is among you, and the love which you have toward all the saints, don't cease to give thanks for you, making mention of you in my prayers, that the God of our Lord Jesus Christ, the Father of glory, may give to you a spirit of wisdom and revelation in the knowledge of him, having the eyes of your hearts enlightened, that you may know what is the hope of his calling, and what are the riches of the glory of his inheritance in the saints. (Ephesians 1:13–18 WEB)

The Greek word *Arrabon* means "deposit, down payment, earnest money, security, and pledge." In modern Greek, the word *Arrabona* means "an engagement ring." Fifty days after Jesus was resurrected on the feast of Pentecost in Acts 2, the Holy Spirit was given as a seal of promise, a deposit to the final inheritance of the earth. The full payment is to come when the marriage feast begins. When Jesus asked us to eat of His body—the eucharist—and drink of His blood, the wine, we are accepting Jesus's betrothal and our salvation.

The reason God uses marriage language is because this union between a man and woman becoming one with God is the most sacred of sacraments. Shalanda, my publisher's SA (Senior Accounting) manager, said it perfectly: "It requires a great amount of feat (courage, skill, strength) and an immense amount of communication, loyalty, trust, and most importantly, love!" This is what Christians are accepting with Jesus's engagement ring, and how we receive our salvation and everlasting life.

The Greek word *Elpis* means "hope, expectation, prospect, and calling."

"That you may know what is the hope of his calling." (Ephesians 1:18 WEB)

In this sentence, Apostle Paul is telling us that God's calling, or *Elpis*, is God's hope and expectations he has for us! God has hope in you! He can hardly wait to be with all His children and give them their inheritance.

I saw a new heaven and a new earth: for the first heaven and the first earth have passed away, and the sea is no more. I saw the holy city, New Jerusalem, coming down out of heaven from God, prepared like a bride adorned for her husband. I heard a loud voice out of heaven saying,

"Behold, God's dwelling is with people, and he will dwell with them, and they will be his people, and God himself will be with them as their God. He will wipe away every tear from their eyes. Death will be no more; neither will there be mourning, nor crying, nor pain, any more. The first things have passed away."

He who sits on the throne said, "Behold, I am making all things new." He said, "Write, for these words of God are faithful and true." He said to me, "I am the Alpha and the Omega, the Beginning and the End. I will give freely to him who is thirsty from the spring of the water of life. He who overcomes, I will give him these things. I will be his God, and he will be my son. But for the cowardly, unbelieving, sinners, abominable, murderers, sexually immoral, sorcerers, idolaters, and all liars, their part is in the lake that burns with fire and sulfur, which is the second death."

One of the seven angels who had the seven bowls, who were loaded with the seven last plagues came, and he spoke with me, saying, "Come here. I will show you the wife, the Lamb's bride." He carried me away in the Spirit to a great and high mountain, and showed me the holy city, Jerusalem, coming down out of heaven from God, having the glory of God. Her light was like a most precious stone, as if it were a jasper stone, clear as crystal; having a great and high wall; having twelve gates, and at the gates twelve angels; and names written on them, which are the names of the twelve tribes of the children of Israel. On the east were three gates; and on the north three gates; and on the south three gates; and on the west three gates. The wall of the city had twelve foundations, and on them twelve names of the twelve Apostles of the Lamb. He who spoke with me had for a measure a golden reed to measure the city, its gates, and its walls. The city is square, and its length is as great as its width. He measured the city with the reed, twelve thousand twelve stadia. Its length, width, and height are equal. Its wall is one hundred forty-four cubits, by the measure of a man, that is, of an angel. The construction of its wall was jasper. The city was pure gold, like pure glass. The foundations of the city's wall were adorned with all kinds of precious stones. The first foundation was jasper; the second, sapphire; the third, chalcedony; the fourth, emerald; the fifth, sardonyx; the sixth, sardius; the seventh, chrysolite; the eighth, beryl; the ninth, topaz; the tenth, chrysoprase; the eleventh, jacinth; and the twelfth, amethyst. The twelve gates were twelve pearls. Each one of the gates was made of one pearl. The street of the city was pure gold, like transparent glass. I saw no temple in it, for the Lord God, the Almighty, and the Lamb, are its temple. The city has no need for the sun or moon to shine, for the very glory of God illuminated it, and its lamp is the Lamb. The nations will walk in its light. The kings of the earth bring the glory and honor of the nations into it. Its gates will in no way be shut by day (for there will be no night there), and they shall bring the glory and the honor of the nations into it so that they may enter. There will in no way enter into it anything profane, or one who causes an abomination or a lie, but only those who are written in the Lamb's book of life. (Revelation 21 WEB)

This new holy city of Jerusalem is filled with precious gems. These gems represent the twelve tribes of Israel. Each tribe has its own gemstone, the high priests wore a breast plate during his ministry with twelve stones on it called an Urim and Thummim.

> You shall set in it settings of stones, four rows of stones: a row of ruby, topaz, and beryl shall be the first row; and the second row a turquoise, a sapphire, and an emerald; and the third row a jacinth, an agate, and an amethyst; and the fourth row a chrysolite, an onyx, and a jasper. They shall be enclosed in gold in their settings. The stones shall be according to the names of the children of Israel, twelve, according to their names; like the engravings of a signet, everyone according to his name, they shall be for the twelve tribes. (Exodus 28:17–21 WEB)

Here is a list of the tribes and their stones: Benjamin, jasper; Dan, sapphire; Asher, chalcedony; Judah, emerald; Joseph, sardonyx; Reuben, sardius; Gad, chrysolite; Zebulun, beryl; Simeon, topaz; Naphtali, chrysoprase; Levi, jacinth; Issachar, amethyst.

In the scripture, it says, "The city has no need for the sun or moon to shine, for the very glory of God illuminated it" (Revelation 21:23 WEB). Just imagine a new world so bright that everything will glow like a rainbow. This light is God's love illuminating and overflowing with pure radiant joy for His people, His promise, and His new world.

May Jesus rejoice over you during this glorious wedding feast when we will see God face-to-face. Amen.

A LASTING IMPRESSION

> But now Yahweh who created you, Jacob,
> and he who formed you, Israel, says: "Don't be
> afraid, for I have redeemed you. I have called you
> by your name. You are mine." (Isaiah 43:1 WEB)

> Behold, I have engraved you on the palms
> of my hands. Your walls are continually before
> me. (Isaiah 49:16 WEB)

The Bible is God's word; the truth is written in Scripture, and He gives us a lasting impression to everyone who reads, conforms, and believes in it. These forever impressions are that we belong to Him and we are engraved on the palms of His hands. When He created you in your mother's womb, He gave you unique fingerprints. It all starts when you are an inch in size, about one month after conception. When your fingers form epidermis pads, this creates a foundation for fingerprints. This also happens on the toes for toeprints. Then as you grow and touch your mother's womb, it gives your fingers faint lines and impressions with arches, loops, and whorls unique to anyone else in the whole world.

So when God says that He has engraved you on the palms of His hands, that means that your unique fingerprints are indelible marks on His hand that can't be removed ever. God will continually take care of you forever.

The final chapter in Revelation is Jesus telling us that He will be with His father on the throne and His servants, worshiping them both. In the new kingdom with rivers of living waters and the tree of life bearing fruit that heals all the nations. Jesus addresses His final prophecy and blessings to those who keep God's words and have Christ written on their foreheads. Oh, what joy this will be to finally be with our Lord and Savior for all eternity!

He showed me a river of water of life, clear as crystal, proceeding out of the throne of God and of the Lamb, in the middle of its street. On this side of the river and on that was the tree of life, bearing twelve kinds of fruits, yielding its fruit every month. The leaves of the tree were for the healing of the nations. There will be no curse anymore. The throne of God and of the Lamb will be in it, and his servants will serve him. They will see his face, and his name will be on their foreheads. There will be no night, and they need no lamp light or sun light; for the Lord God will illuminate them. They will reign forever and ever.

He said to me, "These words are faithful and true. The Lord God of the spirits of the prophets sent his angel to show to his bondservants the things which must happen soon."

"Behold, I come quickly. Blessed is he who keeps the words of the prophecy of this book."

Now I, John, am the one who heard and saw these things. When I heard and saw, I fell down to worship before the feet of the angel who had shown me these things. He said to me, "See you don't do it! I am a fellow bondservant with you and with your brothers, the prophets, and with those who keep the words of this book. Worship God." He said to me, "Don't seal up the words of the prophecy of this book, for the time is at hand.

He who acts unjustly, let him act unjustly still. He who is filthy, let him be filthy still. He who is righteous, let him do righteousness still. He who is holy, let him be holy still."

"Behold, I come quickly. My reward is with me, to repay to each man according to his work. I am the Alpha and the Omega, the First and the Last, the Beginning and the End. Blessed are those who do his commandments, that they may have the right to the tree of life and may enter in by the gates into the city. Outside are the dogs, the sorcerers, the sexually immoral, the murderers, the idolaters, and everyone who loves and practices falsehood. I, Jesus, have sent my angel to testify these things to you for the assemblies. I am the root and the offspring of David, the Bright and Morning Star."

The Spirit and the bride say, "Come!" He who hears, let him say, "Come!" He who is thirsty, let him come. He who desires, let him take the water of life freely. I testify to everyone who hears the words of the prophecy of this book, if anyone adds to them, may God add to him the plagues which are written in this book. If anyone takes away from the words of the book of this prophecy, may God take away his part from the tree of life, and out of the holy city, which are written in this book. He who testifies these things says, "Yes, I come quickly."

Amen! Yes, come, Lord Jesus.

The grace of the Lord Jesus Christ be with all the saints. Amen." (Revelation 22 WEB)

When the eternal Eden is here, mankind will have come full circle and see God and Jesus face-to-face. We will all be singing "Holy, Holy, Holy" to our Lord every day forever and ever. This lasting impression is the ultimate climax of every true child of God, and God will be free to live His own life. There will be no great divide, no boundary between life and death, no more death: only life. A new world united with divine communion of love and life, all sharing in the glory of God, all His creation, and the glory of Jesus's reign as our new king forever. Amen.

GOD'S DWELLING PLACE

God lives in heaven and in His kingdom and in the universe as far as the eye can see and beyond your imagination. God is all in all. Jesus also said that the kingdom of God is within you.

> "Neither will they say, 'Look, here!' or, 'Look, there!' for behold, God's Kingdom is within you." (Luke 17:21 WEB)

The kingdom of God is not simply what awaits us at some time in the future; God's dwelling place is also in your soul, as deep and inward as far as your imagination can take you—the innermost hidden center of yourself. The mysteries of the vast infinite universe and the vast infinite depths of our souls are beyond our comprehension. If we reflect on this a little deeper, we will realize that if God lives in heaven and in His kingdom and lives within you, then you are God's heaven! Your soul is God's soul because we were made in the image of God.

> For God created man to be immortal and made him to be an image of his own eternity. The righteous, because they are made in the image of God, can rest in the full hope of eternal life. (Wisdom of Solomon 2:23, CPDV)

Yahweh God formed man from the dust of the ground and breathed into his nostrils the breath of life; and man became a living soul. (Genesis 2:7 WEB)

So let's just imagine God living in our soul in a bright, beautiful, translucent place full of precious gems and rainbows. A place full of love, peace, and joy. A place with rivers of living waters springing forth and reflecting yourself in the way God created you to be. Saint Teresa of Avila said, "I began to think of the soul as if it were a castle made of a single diamond or a very clear crystal, in which there are many rooms, just as in Heaven there are many mansions."

As we contemplate God in prayer, we journey to this place to seek a deeper meaning of ourselves with God. In Scripture, Jesus said that He prepared this place for you in His Fathers mansion.

> "Don't let your heart be troubled. Believe in God. Believe also in me. In my Father's house are many homes. If it weren't so, I would have told you. I am going to prepare a place for you. If I go and prepare a place for you, I will come again, and will receive you to myself; that where I am, you may be there also. You know where I go, and you know the way." … "If a man loves me, he will keep my word. My Father will love him, and we will come to him, and make our home with him." (John 14:1–4, 23 WEB)

The meaning for the Greek word for mansions is "house, resting-places, or dwellings." A home is a symbol of your personal identity and reflects the dwelling place of your own soul, heart, and mind. Your home also includes everyone in your household, including animals and the flock of people you associate with. God protects your home and takes this sacred dwelling place very seriously. Jesus gave us this key to protect our dwelling place in Matthew 16:19 (WEB), "I will give to you the keys of the Kingdom of Heaven, and whatever you bind on earth will have been bound in heaven; and whatever you release on earth will have been released in heaven."

What Jesus is saying here is that whatever we covet, whatever we yearn to possess that does not belong to us, should be banished and to keep what is rightfully ours. The key is that God will simply forbid or permit what is bound or released in heaven by His indisputable authority. God helps us Christians identify the dwelling place of our own soul, revealing our true identity; our true and rightful path in life is what we keep, what we bind on Earth will be bound in our soul.

Everything about God, Jesus, and the Holy Spirit is mystical, and those with faith know in their hearts that the Trinity is real; and as we deepen our connectedness to God, we deepen our understanding of God's reality in us and us within all His creation and where we fit in. The Holy Spirit helps us reveal who we really are in the eyes of God and not our false self—to take off our mask, so to speak, revealing our true identity. He does this through redemption, teaches us the meaning of sacred Scripture, how to apply God's word, and work toward His divine plan of salvation.

> And the Spirit of the LORD will come upon thee, and thou shalt prophesy with them, and shalt be turned into another man. (1 Samuel 10:6 KJV)

> But you are not in the flesh but in the Spirit, if it is so that the Spirit of God dwells in you. But if any man doesn't have the Spirit of Christ, he is not his. If Christ is in you, the body is dead because of sin, but the spirit is alive because of righteousness. (Romans 8:9–10 WEB)

Through prayer and contemplation, we learn to listen to God's still small voice inside us and yearn to seek Him inside our soul, our innermost hidden center of ourselves. But the question always arises, "I am not worthy, oh Lord." This is true, for humans are sinful by nature and can never be perfect. But I think that God loves us unconditionally. He allows us to enter this inner sanctuary with all our imperfections, infirmities, iniquities, and things that we covet.

God desires for us to seek Him in a way that becomes more important than our imperfections, infirmities, iniquities, and the things that we covet. He knows that the more we seek Him, the less attention we give to ourselves, and the less time we will spend feeding our egos, our grudges, our addictions, our sins, or our scaly pet we have hidden in the closet.

Shame will hold us back because we will never be perfect or never measure up. The only one who is perfect is God, and so the first thing He tells us is that with Him, through perseverance and redemption, prayer and contemplation, we can pursue a right and just path during our lifetime.

seeing that you seek a proof of Christ who speaks in me; who toward you is not weak, but is powerful in you. For he was crucified through weakness, yet he lives through the power of God. For we also are weak in him, but we will live with him through the power of God toward you. Examine your own selves, whether you are in the faith. Test your own selves. (2 Corinthians 13:3–5 WEB)

My son, if you will receive my words,
and store up my commandments within you,
so as to turn your ear to wisdom,
and apply your heart to understanding;
yes, if you call out for discernment,
and lift up your voice for understanding;
if you seek her as silver,
and search for her as for hidden treasures:
then you will understand the fear of Yahweh,
and find the knowledge of God.
For Yahweh gives wisdom.
Out of his mouth comes knowledge and understanding.

He lays up sound wisdom for the upright.
He is a shield to those who walk in integrity,
that he may guard the paths of justice,
and preserve the way of his saints.
Then you will understand righteousness
and justice,
equity and every good path.
For wisdom will enter into your heart.
Knowledge will be pleasant to your soul.
Discretion will watch over you.
Understanding will keep you,
to deliver you from the way of evil,
from the men who speak perverse things,
who forsake the paths of uprightness,
to walk in the ways of darkness,
who rejoice to do evil,
and delight in the perverseness of evil,
who are crooked in their ways,
and wayward in their paths,
to deliver you from the strange woman,
even from the foreigner who flatters with
her words,
who forsakes the friend of her youth,
and forgets the covenant of her God;
for her house leads down to death,
her paths to the departed spirits.
None who go to her return again,
neither do they attain to the paths of life.
So you may walk in the way of good men,
and keep the paths of the righteous.
For the upright will dwell in the land.
The perfect will remain in it.
But the wicked will be cut off from the land.
The treacherous will be rooted out of it.
(Proverbs 2, WEB)

Look at the little children playing on a playground, the small child dancing around in circles singing; they seem to not have a care in this world, just joy and laughter. Jesus said that this is how we are to humble ourselves to enter into God's dwelling place.

> "Most certainly I tell you, unless you turn and become as little children, you will in no way enter into the Kingdom of Heaven. Whoever therefore humbles himself as this little child is the greatest in the Kingdom of Heaven." (Matthew 18:3–4 WEB)

> In that day you will know that I am in my Father, and you in me, and I in you. One who has my commandments and keeps them, that person is one who loves me. One who loves me will be loved by my Father, and I will love him, and will reveal myself to him. (John 14:20–21 WEB)

So God lives inside my soul, and I am His heaven; then my heaven holds all who are dear to my heart—my loved ones, people, and pets that have gone before me. And on Earth, my heaven is right here where my home is with all my loving family, friends, and pets. My heaven is full of peace, love, and joy thanks to our loving God who freed me from my chains and redeemed me. I thank God every day for His loving care and for the gracious gifts of life that He gives me. So what's in your heaven? Is it empty or full of life? May the Lord bless you and keep you in His care. Amen.

> "The Lord bless you and keep you; The Lord make His face shine upon you, And be gracious to you; The Lord lift up His countenance upon you, And give you peace." (Numbers 6:24–26 NKJV)

GOD'S DANCE

As we deepen our connectedness to God and deepen our understanding of God's reality in us, we learn where we fit into His world. God loves life and loves us living in it so much that He invites us to dance with Him. Once we find God living inside our soul—His dwelling place that is full of precious gems and rainbows—and learn to release what does not belong to us, we begin to work and move in harmony and in unison with God, Jesus, and the Holy Spirit.

Perichoresis is a Greek word that means "around, to give way." In this unison, we rotate around precisely and elegantly with the Trinity, creating a choreographed dance and move as one with each other. I enjoy watching the flocks of Canadian geese fly in unison every fall and springtime; it is like they have rehearsed the flight into a choreographed dance. Or a field of grass that blows freely in the wind; it looks like ocean waves—even schools of fish swim in unison. God invites those of us who are zealous to do His will to dance with Him in this life and in eternal life forever. We are trained by saving grace.

> For the grace of God that brings salvation has appeared to all men, teaching us that, denying ungodliness and worldly lusts, we should live soberly, righteously, and godly in the present age, looking for the blessed hope and glorious appearing of our great God and Savior Jesus Christ, who gave Himself for us, that He might redeem us from every lawless deed and purify for Himself

His own special people, zealous for good works. (Titus 2:11–14 NKJV)

I often repeat to myself this poetry phase,

It's not my time, it's God's time.
It's not my world, it's God's world.
It's not my life, it's God life.

Dancing with a purpose just as the little child dancing in circles and singing joyfully, is a form of praising our Lord. Jeremiah and King David understood this and wrote about it like poetry.
Yahweh appeared of old to me, saying,

"Yes, I have loved you with an everlasting love. Therefore, I have drawn you with loving kindness. I will build you again, and you will be built, O virgin of Israel. You will again be adorned with your tambourines, and will go out in the dances of those who make merry." (Jeremiah 31:3-4, WEB)

"Their soul will be as a watered garden. They will not sorrow any more at all. Then the virgin will rejoice in the dance; the young men and the old together; for I will turn their mourning into joy, and will comfort them, and make them rejoice from their sorrow. I will satiate the soul of the priests with fatness, and my people will be satisfied with my goodness," says Yahweh. (Jeremiah 31:12–14 WEB)

Praise Yahweh! Sing to Yahweh a new song, his praise in the assembly of the saints. Let Israel rejoice in him who made them. Let the children of Zion be joyful in their King. Let them praise his name in the dance! Let them sing praises to him with tambourine and harp! For Yahweh takes pleasure in his people. He crowns the humble with salvation. Let the saints rejoice in honor. Let them sing for joy on their beds. (Psalm 149:1–5 WEB)

Praise Yah! Praise God in his sanctuary! Praise him in his heavens for his acts of power! Praise him for his mighty acts! Praise him according to his excellent greatness! Praise him with the sounding of the trumpet! Praise him with harp and lyre! Praise him with tambourine and dancing! Praise him with stringed instruments and flute! Praise him with loud cymbals! Praise him with resounding cymbals! Let everything that has breath praise Yah! Praise Yah! (Psalm 150 WEB)

You have turned my mourning into dancing for me. You have removed my sackcloth, and clothed me with gladness. (Psalm 30:11 WEB)

Oh clap your hands, all you nations. Shout to God with the voice of triumph! For Yahweh Most High is awesome. He is a great King over all the earth. He subdues nations under us, and peoples under our feet. He chooses our inheritance for us, the glory of Jacob whom he loved. Selah. God has gone up with a shout, Yahweh with the sound of a trumpet. Sing praises to God! Sing praises! Sing praises to our King! Sing praises! For God is the King of all the earth. Sing praises with understanding. God reigns over the nations. God sits on his holy throne. The princes of the peoples are gathered together, the people of the God of

Abraham. For the shields of the earth belong to God. He is greatly exalted! (Psalm 47 WEB)

David danced before Yahweh with all his might; and David was clothed in a linen ephod. So David and all the house of Israel brought up Yahweh's ark with shouting, and with the sound of the trumpet.

As Yahweh's ark came into David's city, Michal the daughter of Saul looked out through the window, and saw king David leaping and dancing before Yahweh. (2 Samuel 6:14–16 WEB)

For everything there is a season, and a time for every purpose under heaven:
a time to be born, and a time to die;
a time to plant, and a time to pluck up that which is planted;
a time to kill, and a time to heal;
a time to break down, and a time to build up;
a time to weep, and a time to laugh;
a time to mourn, and a time to dance;
(Ecclesiastes 3:1–4 WEB)

CHAPTER 2

God's Angels

CHANGING TIDES

Before I get started on this chapter on angels, I would like to thank my nephew, Mark Grater, for taking the challenge to draw Revelation and angel images for this book. As I am writing this book, I discovered how difficult it is to get these types of images. It is not like I can just take a picture of Jesus coming down from the sky riding a white horse, or of a seven-headed beast, or of Satan trying to get into heaven. This would take someone with extraordinary artistic creativity!

One day, my sister and I were doing a Bible study at my home, and Mark called her on the cell phone. I have not spoken to Mark in years. He is in prison and is limited to outside contact. He was reading one of my books and said that he was enjoying it. It came to me that he is an extremely talented artist, so I asked his mother to email him and see if he would be interested in helping Jesus and me with this difficult task. Well, he jumped at the opportunity and said yes.

You see, Mark and I are somewhat similar in our past situations, and we have both turned the tides on our lives for a richer and better life. Mark is a hotshot forest firefighter, and I am a published author. Jesus has reversed our misfortunes and given us a chance to better ourselves.

"For my thoughts are not your thoughts,
and your ways are not my ways," says Yahweh.
"For as the heavens are higher than the
earth, so are my ways higher than your ways, and

my thoughts than your thoughts." (Isaiah 55:8–9 WEB)

Our lives are richer, healthier, and productive. We have found our place in life and have learned that what we do matters, and that we can help make this world a better place. It is so exciting that Jesus is giving us this chance to work together!

> "For I know the thoughts that I think toward you," says Yahweh, "thoughts of peace, and not of evil, to give you hope and a future." (Jeremiah 29:11 WEB)

I hope and pray that our relationship grows into a fruitful future, for the best is yet to come.

Thank you, Mark!
Love, Auntie Karen

HEAVENLY HOSTS

Heavenly hosts are angels. God created them primarily to serve and worship Him. Heavenly hosts refer to the army of angels that are equipped with many tasks. The Hebrew word for angels is *mal'ak*, and in Greek it is *angelos*. Both words mean messenger.

But the angel said to him, "Don't be afraid, Zacharias, because your request has been heard. Your wife, Elizabeth, will bear you a son, and you shall call his name John. (Luke 1:13 WEB)

The angel said to her, "Don't be afraid, Mary, for you have found favor with God." (Luke 1:30 WEB)

They are angelical creatures, and not human beings or omniscient, like God. They not only carry messages to humans, but they are mediators of many kinds.

"You received the law as it was ordained by angels and didn't keep it!" (Acts 7:53 WEB)

Then why is there the law? It was added because of transgressions, until the offspring should come to whom the promise has been made. It was ordained through angels by the hand of a mediator. (Galatians 3:19 WEB)

This is the Revelation of Jesus Christ, which God gave him to show to his servants the things which must happen soon, which he sent and made known by his angel to his servant, John. (Revelation 1:1 WEB)

Not all angels are identified with wings like the cherubim and seraphim. The Bible often describes these messengers as men in human form.

Yahweh appeared to him by the oaks of Mamre, as he sat in the tent door in the heat of the day. He lifted up his eyes and looked and saw that three men stood near him. When he saw them, he ran to meet them from the tent door, and bowed himself to the earth, and said, "My lord, if now I have found favor in your sight, please don't go away from your servant." (Genesis 18:1–3 WEB)

There are archangels, thrones angels, and guardian angels. There are angels of virtues, principalities, dominions, and powers. There are angels that only sing to God, there are angels that only worship Him, and there are fallen angels.

Of all the creatures created by God, angels are high in rank because of their intellectual understanding of the knowledge of God's will and to carry out that will. Their higher intellect is more universal, and they understand God's cause with remarkable dignity for that divine purpose and direction. They are holy and, by their virtue, are given a greater share in the order of divine governing, such as keeping track of us human beings and keeping a close eye on Satan and the angels that have fallen in rank.

There are a multitude of angels, and we don't have any way of knowing how many there are.

> But you have come to Mount Zion, and to the city of the living God, the heavenly Jerusalem, and to innumerable multitudes of angels. (Hebrews 12:22 WEB)

The Bible only mentions a few by their name.

To understand how the angels acquired their name, you must understand the Jewish tradition. The oldest Hebrew text found was the Law of Moses, also known as the Torah or the Septuagint. It is the first five books of the Bible. Egyptian writings have been found 3,000 BC, and Hinduism scripture is dated 1,500 BC. Jewish texts are a major literary element that have had a profound influence on Christianity.

Most people during the Old Testament times could not read or write, so the Rabbi teachers would read to a group of people in a way of a story that the people could understand. If the story was about faith, then he would start the story out with the name of an angel like Uzziel because in Hebrew, it means "strength of God." We receive great strength from God through our faith. If he started the story out with the name of the angel Selaphiel it would be a story about prayer because in Hebrew, that name means "the prayer of God." If he used the angel's name Gabriel, then the story would reveal a revelation of God's because Gabriel in Hebrew means "God is my strength," and Gabriel delivers great messages announcing an upcoming wonderful event from God, like the Virgin Mary conceiving Jesus. Old Jewish text are written with more angel names in them, like the Torah, Enoch, Talmud, and the mystical Kabbalistic text.

In the next few chapters, I have written about several angels that the Bible does not mention by name, but I have collected the appropriate angel name with the appropriate scripture. Just keep in mind that these angels are very important to the Jewish people, and Jesus is a very important rabbi to Christians.

LET THERE BE LIGHT

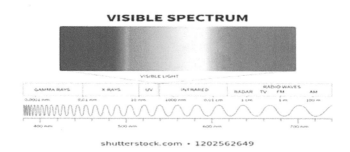

VISIBLE SPECTRUM

shutterstock.com • 1202562649

Light plays a fundamental role in God's creations.

> God said, "Let there be light," and there was
> light. (Genesis 1:3 WEB)

The energy from this light fuels our planet and the universe, and even dark matter has light in it called neutrinos. Light is a symbol of spirituality and is associated with God's wisdom and truth. In Scripture, the word *enlightened* means "to give knowledge or insight to someone."

> In him was life, and the life was the light of
> men. (John 1:4 WEB)

Light signifies salvation from the darkness of sin.

> Then spake Jesus again unto them, saying,
> I am the light of the world: he that followeth me
> shall not walk in darkness, but shall have the light
> of life. (John 8:12 KJV)

Light is composed of photons that make up electromagnetic waves, and these waves are responsible for the transduction of light into nervous impulses. These energy fields are also known as auras. Auras emanate a glow of light around people, living things, planets, moons, and even angels. This light generated reflects the current state of a person's emotional, mental, physical, and spiritual state. Lighter color auras emanate joy and peace, while dark auras show negative emotions like sorrow and anger. Auras in angels reveal information about what kind of angel it is. Angel's light rays vibrate at different electromagnetic energy frequencies in the universe; they attract and communicate with other angels that have similar kinds of energy wavelengths. The transcending or metaphysical system of angel colors correspond to the visible light spectrum that consists of the light we see from a rainbow. There are seven basic light rays: white, purple, blue, green, yellow, red, and pink. Each color represents a different meaning.

White angel light rays clear away confusion to achieve wisdom, harmony, and purity so one can understand a revelation from God and become more holy and faithful to Jesus.

Purple angel light rays help with transformation of mercy. It motivates people to pray for forgiveness and encourages them to forgive others.

Blue angel light rays give courage, strength, protection, faith, and the power to be overcomers.

Green angel light rays are for healing and prosperity to bring people closer to God so they can experience peace and joy.

Yellow angel light rays represent the wisdom needed for decision making, solving problems, creative inspirations, and illuminating one's soul with beautiful thoughts.

Red angel light rays represent wise service for God, discernment, discovering, and developing distinctive services and talents that God has given you to focus on ways to making this world a better place.

Pink angel light rays correspond to the heart with love and peace, helping with forgiveness and compassion for others, builds self-confidence, and maintain a loving relationship with God and others.

Gravitation pulls light to earth and pulls light through our galaxy. Light travels at 186,000 miles per second, and because angels use this electromagnetic energy field, that may be why we cannot see them except when God orders them to slow down and make an earthy visit.

SERAPHIM ANGELS

Seraphim angels guard God's throne, singing and praising God. They are highest in rank and closest to God. *Seraphim* in Hebrew means "burning ones" or "to burn." Their bright light that burns from within them manifest a burning passion for God. They have six wings and use two wings to cover their feet, showing humility and respect for God; two wings to cover their face, shielding God's great glory; and two wings to fly around His throne.

> In the year that king Uzziah died, I saw the Lord sitting on a throne, high and lifted up; and his train filled the temple. Above him stood the seraphim. Each one had six wings. With two he covered his face. With two he covered his feet. With two he flew. One called to another, and said, "Holy, holy, holy, is Yahweh of Armies! The whole earth is full of his glory!" (Isaiah 6:1–3 WEB)

> He said, "You cannot see my face, for man may not see me and live." (Exodus 33:20 WEB)

The four living creatures, each one of them having six wings, are full of eyes around and within. They have no rest day and night, saying, "Holy, holy, holy is the Lord God, the Almighty, who was and who is and who is to come!" (Revelation 4:8, WEB)

Set me as a seal on your heart, as a seal on your arm; for love is strong as death. Jealousy is as cruel as Sheol. Its flashes are flashes of fire, a very flame of Yahweh. (Song of Solomon 8:6 WEB)

Lucifer was the seraphim angel closest to God because he was the most beautiful and he was the brightest angel. Then he rebelled against God and was casted out of heaven and fell to earth like lightning bolts.

He said to them, "I saw Satan having fallen like lightning from heaven." (Luke 10:18 WEB)

Other Seraphim archangels are Saint Michael, the leader of all angels; Metatron, God's chief record-keeper; Uriel, angel of wisdom; Chamuel, angel of peaceful relationships; and Seraphiel, angel of purification.

While Seraphim angels' main duty is to guard God's throne, they also do heavenly chores, and on special occasions, they will come to Earth on a mission from God. Saint Michael engages in battles of spiritual warfare to protect humans from Satan and demons.

CHERUBIM ANGELS

The ARK of the COVENANT
By Karen Parker

The Cherubim angels protect God's glory no matter what happens in heaven, on Earth, or in the universe. They give glory, honor, and thanks to God for creating humans, animals and others living creatures that God created. They are angels with four wings and are second in the rank of angels.

> When the living creatures give glory, honor, and thanks to him who sits on the throne, to him who lives forever and ever, the twenty-four elders fall down before him who sits on the throne, and worship him who lives forever and ever, and throw their crowns before the throne, saying, "Worthy are you, our Lord and God, the Holy One, to receive the glory, the honor, and the power, for you created all things, and because of your desire they existed, and were created!" (Revelation 4:9–11 WEB)

They have eyes all around them representing that nothing escapes their attention.

> In the middle of the throne, and around the throne were four living creatures full of eyes before and behind. The first creature was like a lion, and the second creature like a calf, and the third creature had a face like a man, and the

fourth was like a flying eagle. (Revelation 4:6–7 WEB)

One of their divine missions from God is to guard the tree of life in the garden of Eden from humans who have fallen to sin.

> So he drove out the man; and he placed cherubim at the east of the garden of Eden, and a flaming sword which turned every way, to guard the way to the tree of life. (Genesis 3:24 WEB)

The cherubim guard God's glory and mercy in heaven; they stay beside Him always. Moses needed a place on Earth for God to manifest for the Israelites to atone their sins, so God gave Moses special instructions on how to build a mercy seat with cherubim to cover the ark of the covenant. This atonement cover symbolized God's mercy for the Israelites to embrace the mercy and forgiveness that God offers them.

> You shall put the covenant which I shall give you into the ark. You shall make a mercy seat of pure gold. Two and a half cubits shall be its length, and a cubit and a half its width. You shall make two cherubim of hammered gold. You shall make them at the two ends of the mercy seat. Make one cherub at the one end, and one cherub at the other end. You shall make the cherubim on its two ends of one piece with the mercy seat. The cherubim shall spread out their wings upward, covering the mercy seat with their wings, with their faces toward one another. The faces of the cherubim shall be toward the mercy seat. You shall put the mercy seat on top of the ark, and in the ark, you shall put the covenant that I will give you. There I will meet with you, and I will tell you from above the mercy seat, from between the

two cherubim which are on the ark of the covenant, all that I command you for the children of Israel. (Exodus 25:16–22 WEB)

and above it cherubim of glory overshadowing the mercy seat, of which things we can't speak now in detail. (Hebrews 9:5 WEB)

Hear us, Shepherd of Israel, you who lead Joseph like a flock, you who sit above the cherubim, shine out. (Psalm 80:1 WEB)

Yahweh reigns! Let the peoples tremble. He sits enthroned among the cherubim. Let the earth be moved. (Psalm 99:1 WEB)

Hezekiah prayed before Yahweh, and said, "Yahweh, the God of Israel, who are enthroned above the cherubim, you are the God, even you alone, of all the kingdoms of the earth." (2 Kings 19:15 WEB)

The prophet Ezekiel had great visions from God displaying these unique and incredible celestial beings:

I looked, and behold, a stormy wind came out of the north: a great cloud, with flashing lightning, and a brightness around it, and out of the middle of it as it were glowing metal, out of the middle of the fire. Out of its center came the likeness of four living creatures. This was their appearance: They had the likeness of a man. Everyone had four faces, and each one of them had four wings. Their feet were straight feet. The sole of their feet was like the sole of a calf's foot; and they sparkled like burnished bronze. They had the hands of a man under their wings on their four sides. The four of them had their faces and their wings like this: Their wings were joined to one another. They didn't turn when they went. Each one went straight forward. (Ezekiel 1:4–9 WEB)

Then I looked, and see, in the expanse that was over the head of the cherubim there appeared above them as it were a sapphire stone, as the appearance of the likeness of a throne. He spoke to the man clothed in linen, and said, "Go in between the whirling wheels, even under the cherub, and fill both your hands with coals of fire from between the cherubim and scatter them over the city.

He went in as I watched. Now the cherubim stood on the right side of the house, when the man went in; and the cloud filled the inner court. Yahweh's glory mounted up from the cherub and stood over the threshold of the house; and the house was filled with the cloud, and the court was full of the brightness of Yahweh's glory. The sound of the wings of the cherubim was heard even to the outer court, as the voice of God Almighty when he speaks.

It came to pass, when he commanded the man clothed in linen, saying, "Take fire from between the whirling wheels, from between the cherubim," that he went in, and stood beside a wheel. The cherub stretched out his hand from between the cherubim to the fire that was between the cherubim, and took some of it, and put it into the hands of him who was clothed in linen, who took it and went out. The form of a man's hand appeared here in the cherubim under their wings.

I looked, and behold, there were four wheels beside the cherubim, one wheel beside one cherub, and another wheel beside another cherub. The appearance of the wheels was like a beryl stone. As for their appearance, the four of them had one likeness, like a wheel within a wheel. When they went, they went in their four directions. They didn't turn as they went, but to the place where the head looked, they followed it. They didn't turn as they went. Their whole body, including their backs, their hands, their wings, and the wheels, were full of eyes all around, even the wheels that the four of them had. As for the wheels, they were called in my hearing, "the whirling wheels". Every one of them had four faces. The first face was the face of the cherub. The second face was the face of a man. The third face was the face of a lion. The fourth was the face of an eagle.

The cherubim mounted up. This is the living creature that I saw by the river Chebar. When the cherubim went, the wheels went beside them; and when the cherubim lifted up their wings to mount up from the earth, the wheels also didn't turn from beside them. When they stood, these stood. When they mounted up, these mounted up with them; for the spirit of the living creature was in them.

Yahweh's glory went out from over the threshold of the house and stood over the cherubim. The cherubim lifted up their wings, and mounted up from the earth in my sight when they went out, with the wheels beside them. Then they stood at the door of the east gate of Yahweh's house; and the glory of the God of Israel was over them above.

This is the living creature that I saw under the God of Israel by the river Chebar; and I knew that they were cherubim. Every one had four faces, and every one four wings. The likeness of the hands of a man was under their wings. As for the likeness of their faces, they were the faces which I saw by the river Chebar their appearances and themselves. They each went straight forward. (Ezekiel 10:1–22 WEB)

EVANGELIST'S ICONS

There are four iconic symbols in Christianity that represent the four Evangelists of Christ for more than 1,500 years. They are the four gospel writers: Matthew, Mark, Luke, and John. The four living creatures are cherubim angels, one like that of a man, one like that of a lion, one like that of a calf, and one like that of an eagle. *Tetramorph* is a Greek word that means "four living beings."

The winged man is Matthew because he opens the New Testament of the four gospels telling of the good news of Christ.

The lion is a symbol of courage and power that Christians receive from God through their royal dignity of Christ.

The calf or ox symbolizes sacrifice, service, and strength for Christians.

The eagle represents Christians able to look into the sun and onto eternity toward their union with God.

These figures also represent the four faces of God and the four elements or domain of God's rule: the man is humanity, the lion is king of the wild animals, the calf is the king of domestic animals, and the eagle is king of the birds.

> Every one them had four faces. The first
> face was the face of the cherub. The second face
> was the face of a man. The third face was the face

of a lion. The fourth was the face of an eagle.
(Ezekiel 10:14 WEB)

> Before the throne was something like a sea
> of glass, similar to crystal. In the middle of the
> throne, and around the throne were four living
> creatures full of eyes before and behind. The first
> creature was like a lion, and the second creature
> like a calf, and the third creature had a face like
> a man, and the fourth was like a flying eagle."
> (Revelation 4:6–7 WEB)

Catholic art has inspired many with these creative creatures of the four gospels writers for over 1,500 years. Through the gospel stories, Christ has been teaching and still is teaching us how to become faithful Christians and inspiring us by helping humanity in this fallen world.

THRONES ANGELS

Thrones angels are concerned with God's justice; His true judgment comes from His throne. The justice in our world has fallen and is corrupted by sinful people. This injustice needs help, and God will send His thrones angels to help us with spiritual wisdom and understanding to take us out the darkness and into His wonderful kingdom. They are third in the rank of angels.

> For this cause, we also, since the day we heard this, don't cease praying and making requests for you, that you may be filled with the knowledge of his will in all spiritual wisdom and understanding, that you may walk worthily of the Lord, to please him in all respects, bearing fruit in every good work and increasing in the knowledge of God, strengthened with all power, according to the might of his glory, for all endurance and perseverance with joy, giving thanks to the Father, who made us fit to be partakers of the inheritance of the saints in light, who delivered us out of the power of darkness, and translated us into the Kingdom of the Son of his love, in

whom we have our redemption, the forgiveness of our sins. He is the image of the invisible God, the firstborn of all creation. For by him all things were created in the heavens and on the earth, visible things and invisible things, whether thrones or dominions or principalities or powers. All things have been created through him and for him. (Colossians 1:9–16 WEB)

The Apostle Paul says that "by our faith, we receive proof of this justice from God."

Now faith is assurance of things hoped for, proof of things not seen. For by this, the elders obtained testimony. By faith, we understand that the universe has been framed by the word of God, so that what is seen has not been made out of things which are visible. (Hebrews 11:1–3 WEB)

There were only two prophets in the Bible that escaped death: Enoch and Elijah. Thrones angels miraculously saved them from the judgment of death.

By faith, Enoch was taken away, so that he wouldn't see death, and he was not found, because God translated him. For he has had testimony given to him that before his translation he had been well pleasing to God. Without faith it is impossible to be well pleasing to him, for he who comes to God must believe that he exists, and that he is a rewarder of those who seek him. (Hebrews 11:5–6 WEB)

Elijah's chariot and horses of fire were thrones angels sent from God to take him to heaven.

As they continued on and talked, behold, a chariot of fire and horses of fire separated them, and Elijah went up by a whirlwind into heaven. Elisha saw it, and he cried, "My father, my father, the chariots of Israel and its horsemen!" (2 Kings 2:11–12 WEB)

God sends armies of thrones angels as white or fiery horses.

Elisha prayed, and said, "Yahweh, please open his eyes, that he may see." Yahweh opened the young man's eyes; and he saw: and behold, the mountain was full of horses and chariots of fire around Elisha. (2 Kings 6:17 WEB)

The armies which are in heaven followed him on white horses, clothed in white, pure, fine linen. (Revelation 19:14 WEB)

Thrones are also known as winds or just flames of fire or tongues of fire.

He makes his messengers winds, and his servants flames of fire. (Psalm 104:4 WEB)

Tongues like fire appeared and were distributed to them, and one sat on each of them. (Acts 2:3 WEB)

The prophet Daniel tells the story of King Nebuchadnezzar dreams of a tree and how he lived like an animal. Daniel interpreted the dreams to King Nebuchadnezzar, saying that God has sent His angels to deliver a massage. God was asking him to exchange his pride for humility and to give God the praises for his riches and not to praise himself. Since thrones angels deliver messages from God concerning His just judgment on sinful people, the watcher and a holy one coming down from the sky were thrones angels.

> I, Nebuchadnezzar, was at rest in my house, and flourishing in my palace. I saw a dream which made me afraid; and the thoughts on my bed and the visions of my head troubled me. (Daniel 4:4–5 WEB)

> "I saw in the visions of my head on my bed, and behold, a watcher and a holy one came down from the sky. He cried aloud, and said this, 'Cut down the tree, and cut off its branches!'" (Daniel 4:13–14 WEB)

Daniel's interpretation:

> it is you, O king, that have grown and become strong; for your greatness has grown, and reaches to the sky, and your dominion to the end of the earth.
> "Whereas the king saw a watcher and a holy one coming down from the sky, and saying, 'Cut down the tree, and destroy it; nevertheless leave the stump of its roots in the earth, even with a band of iron and bronze, in the tender grass of the field, and let it be wet with the dew of the sky. Let his portion be with the animals of the field, until seven times pass over him.'
> "This is the interpretation, O king, and it is the decree of the Most High, which has come on my lord the king: that you shall be driven from men, and your dwelling shall be with the animals of the field. You shall be made to eat grass as oxen, and shall be wet with the dew of the sky, and seven times shall pass over you; until you know

that the Most High rules in the kingdom of men, and gives it to whomever he will. Whereas they commanded to leave the stump of the roots of the tree; your kingdom shall be sure to you, after that you will have known that the heavens do rule. Therefore, O king, let my counsel be acceptable to you, and break off your sins by righteousness, and your iniquities by showing mercy to the poor. Perhaps there may be a lengthening of your tranquility." (Daniel 4:22–27 WEB)

DOMINION ANGELS

Dominion angels are supervisors. They keep track of other angels' work to make sure that their duties are carried out according to God's will. They evoke authority on the lesser-ranked angels and govern God's domain and His universal plans. They are fourth in angel rank.

The archangel Zadkiel is the leading angel of mercy. He is believed to be the angel that helped Abraham deal with his trial of faith when God had asked him to sacrifice his only son. This would have been the most difficult experience for Abraham.

> He said, "Now take your son, your only son, Isaac, whom you love, and go into the land of Moriah. Offer him there as a burnt offering on one of the mountains which I will tell you of. (Genesis 22:2 WEB)

The dominion angels were the ones who carried out God's orders before He destroyed Sodom and Gomorrah with fire and brimstone. These two angels looked like men and helped Abraham's nephew Lot and his family escape safely.

> When the morning came, then the angels hurried Lot, saying, "Get up! Take your wife and your two daughters who are here, lest you be

consumed in the iniquity of the city." (Genesis 19:15 WEB)

Then Yahweh rained on Sodom and on Gomorrah sulfur and fire from Yahweh out of the sky. He overthrew those cities, all the plain, all the inhabitants of the cities, and that which grew on the ground." (Genesis 19:24–25 WEB)

Dominion angels give our world leaders wisdom and keep God's universal laws in order.

He is the image of the invisible God, the firstborn of all creation. For by him all things were created in the heavens and on the earth, visible things and invisible things, whether thrones or dominions or principalities or powers. All things have been created through him and for him. He is before all things, and in him all things are held together. He is the head of the body, the assembly, who is the beginning, the firstborn from the dead, that in all things he might have the preeminence. For all the fullness was pleased to dwell in him, and through him to reconcile all things to himself by him, whether things on the earth or things in the heavens, having made peace through the blood of his cross. (Colossians 1:15–20 WEB)

VIRTUE ANGELS

Virtue means the showing of behavior to the highest moral standards. It is also the seventh highest order of the ninefold celestial hierarchy of angels. Virtue angels govern nature, controlling the elements and the seasons. They also have control of the stars, moon, and sun. Sometimes they are called "spirits in motion" and the "shining ones."

Now about that time, King Herod stretched out his hands to oppress some of the assembly. He killed James, the brother of John, with the sword. When he saw that it pleased the Jews, he proceeded to seize Peter also. This was during the days of unleavened bread. When he had arrested him, he put him in prison, and delivered him to four squads of four soldiers each to guard him, intending to bring him out to the people after the Passover. Peter therefore was kept in the prison, but constant prayer was made by the assembly to God for him. The same night when Herod was about to bring him out, Peter was sleeping between two soldiers, bound with two chains. Guards in front of the door kept the prison.

And behold, an angel of the Lord stood by him, and a light shone in the cell. He struck Peter on the side, and woke him up, saying, "Stand up quickly!" His chains fell off his hands. The angel said to him, "Get dressed and put on your sandals." He did so. He said to him, "Put on your cloak and follow me." And he went out and followed him. He didn't know that what was being done by the angel was real, but thought he saw a vision. When they were past the first and the second guard, they came to the iron gate that leads into the city, which opened to them by itself. They went out, and went down one street, and immediately the angel departed from him. (Acts 12:1–10 WEB)

Virtue angels also inspire people to strengthen their faith in God and provide courage, grace, and valor. God empowers them to perform miracles and for the miracles that people pray for. This brings to my mind a miracle that the virtue angels preformed on my husband on January 17, 2012. He was driving a semitruck with an attached trailer and was crossing a railroad track when a fully loaded forty-foot double-stacked-cars freight train struck him. He lived by the power of these virtue angels. This is the only explanation we can come up with: that an angel was by his side and saved him by the grace of God. This incident changed his life as well as the life of our family!

Jesus answered them, "I told you, and you don't believe. The works that I do in my Father's name, these testify about me." (John 10:25 WEB)

In scripture, Luke tells us of a woman who was healed by just touching Jesus's garment. The angels of virtue recognized her faith was very strong, and as she courageously crawled through that crowd, the angels of virtue helped her to achieve this miracle of the healing from Jesus.

And Jesus said, Somebody hath touched me: for I perceive that virtue is gone out of me. (Luke 8:46 KJV)

far above all rule, authority, power, dominion, and every name that is named, not only in this age, but also in that which is to come. (Ephesians 1:21 WEB)

POWER ANGELS

Power angels are warrior angels; they take part in the spiritual warfare against demons, defending humans and the cosmos. These monarchs help us fight evil spirits and overcome the temptation of sin that demons trigger.

> Praise Yahweh, you angels of his, who are mighty in strength, who fulfill his word, obeying the voice of his word. (Psalm 103:20 WEB)

We are grateful for these powerful angels of Gods, but we are also told in scripture to say alert and guard ourselves form the evil ones that trigger a temptation.

> Flee from youthful lusts; but pursue righteousness, faith, love, and peace with those who call on the Lord out of a pure heart. But refuse foolish and ignorant questionings, knowing that they generate strife. The Lord's servant must not quarrel, but be gentle toward all, able to teach, patient, in gentleness correcting those who oppose him: perhaps God may give them repentance leading to a full knowledge of the truth,

and they may recover themselves out of the devil's snare, having been taken captive by him to his
will. (2 Timothy 2:22–26 WEB)

Samael is an archangel known to be the chief angel of darkness
in Talmudic lore. The name *Samael* in Hebrew means "venom of
God, poison of God or blindness of God." In the Talmudic lore,
Samael is a figure who is the accuser, seducer, destroyer, and is defi-
nitely one of the fallen angels. He keeps the power angels busy.

They shall not dwell in your land, lest they
make you sin against me, for if you serve their
gods, it will surely be a snare to you. (Exodus
23:33 WEB)

But those who are determined to be rich fall
into a temptation, a snare, and many foolish and
harmful lusts, such as drown men in ruin and
destruction. (1 Timothy 6:9 WEB)

Power angels are intelligent, and their harmonious disposition
gives them the perfect character to deliver divine forces of action to
restore God's order wherever it is threatened by evil forces.

He is the image of the invisible God, the
firstborn of all creation. For by him all things
were created in the heavens and on the earth, visible things and invisible things, whether thrones
or dominions or principalities or *powers*. All
things have been created through him and for
him. He is before all things, and in him all things
are held together. He is the head of the body,
the assembly, who is the beginning, the firstborn
from the dead, that in all things he might have
the preeminence. For all the fullness was pleased
to dwell in him, and through him to reconcile

all things to himself by him, whether things on the earth or things in the heavens, having made peace through the blood of his cross. (Colossians 1:15–20 WEB)

PRINCIPALITY ANGELS

Principality angels are rulers that preside over divine ministry. They work closely with people to help them with prayer, spiritual direction, wisdom, and guide the nation's leaders. Churches benefit greatly for their services while they guide the congregation with inspirational ways to deliver God's message and create bonds between them and their creator.

> He is the image of the invisible God, the firstborn of all creation. For by him all things were created in the heavens and on the earth, visible things and invisible things, whether thrones or dominions or principalities or powers. All things have been created through him and for him. He is before all things, and in him all things are held together. (Colossians 1:15–17 WEB)

These angels are massive in size. They tower over cities and nations to protect people while engaging in military affairs. They can perform miracles to strengthen one's faith and grow closer to God. They help spiritual directors with the insight of awareness and understanding.

Spiritual direction, spiritual discipline, and the practice of contemplation heals the soul. Sister Rita and Sister Regina from Emmaus House dedicate their lives to guide and help people explore matters of the soul, to help one see how powerful their faith can be and keeps them close to God. My spiritual director, Sister Regina, keeps me focused on my spiritual journey with Jesus. For me, she listens intently to my many stories of mystical and divine encounters. These stories are not meant to be told to anyone. She attempts to helps me learn and grow in a relationship with God and to cultivate my life attuned to living with the spirit of God. She helps me develop a deeper awareness with the spiritual aspects of being human.

In five years, she has taken me to many retreats, she has offered several daily contemplation resources, took me through seven complete Bible studies. She just gave me a new Bible written by Bishop Barren called "The Word on Fire," and now we have started "The Bible in a Year" with Father Mike Schmitz. Thank you, Sister Regina, from the bottom of my heart to the top of my soul!

Principality angels also work in the heavenly realm to give us incredible views of God's celestial gifts like comets; meteor showers; aurora borealis; and this year on December 21, 2020, was the Christmas Star, last seen eight hundred years ago. This star was actually the alignment of two planets with Earth: Jupiter and Saturn. As they came to overlap each other, it appeared in the sky as the star of David, just like it did when Jesus was born. This star brings light to the world and peace to a people in need of a savior. Here is a picture of the planets and the star taken by Greg Hogan Photography on that wonderful night.

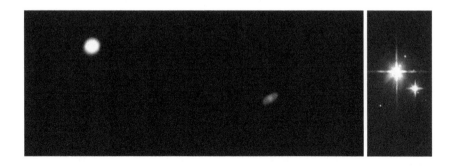

Another wondrous sight was the NEOWISE Comet. It traveled through our atmosphere for about two weeks in July of this year 2020. This comet only orbits near earth every 6,688 years! Here is an incredible photo taken by Abe Snider Photography.

There are also celestial bodies and terrestrial bodies; but the glory of the celestial differs from that of the terrestrial. There is one glory of the sun, another glory of the moon, and another glory of the stars; for one star differs from another star in glory. So also is the resurrection of the dead. The body is sown perishable; it is raised imperishable. (1 Corinthians 15:40–42 WEB)

Now faith is assurance of things hoped for, proof of things not seen. For by this, the elders obtained testimony. By faith, we understand that the universe has been framed by the word of God, so that what is seen has not been made out of things which are visible. (Hebrews 11:1–3 WEB)

GUARDIAN ANGELS

Guardian angels work closest to humans. They don't just protect us from demons and harmful situations; they also strengthen and guide us to have the courage to confront our challenges and inspire us toward God's goals.

> For he will put his angels in charge of you,
> to guard you in all your ways. They will bear you
> up in their hands, so that you won't dash your
> foot against a stone. (Psalm 91:11–12 WEB)

According to Jesus, we receive a guardian angel at birth.

> See that you don't despise one of these little
> ones, for I tell you that in heaven their angels
> always see the face of my Father who is in heaven.
> (Matthew 18:10 WEB)

The guardian angel prayer: "O Angel of God, my Guardian dear, To whom God's love, commits me here, ever this day, be at my side, to light and guard, to rule and guide. Amen."

These guardian messengers also serve as a reminder of God's care for us and the plans that He has for us. In the story of Jacob's ladder, Jacob saw guardian angels ascending and descending on a ladder or stairway from heaven to Earth. Even though Jacob tricked his father into giving him the birthrights instead of the eldest brother, Esau, God loved Jacob and chose him to be the father of all nations, the father of the twelve tribes of Israel.

Jacob went out from Beersheba and went toward Haran. He came to a certain place, and stayed there all night, because the sun had set. He took one of the stones of the place, and put it under his head, and lay down in that place to sleep. He dreamed and saw a stairway set upon the earth, and its top reached to heaven. Behold, the angels of God were ascending and descending on it. Behold, Yahweh stood above it, and said, "I am Yahweh, the God of Abraham your father, and the God of Isaac. I will give the land you lie on to you and to your offspring. Your offspring will be as the dust of the earth, and you will spread abroad to the west, and to the east, and to the north, and to the south. In you and in your offspring, all the families of the earth will be blessed. Behold, I am with you, and will keep you, wherever you go, and will bring you again into this land. For I will not leave you until I have done that which I have spoken of to you."

Jacob awakened out of his sleep, and he said, "Surely Yahweh is in this place, and I didn't know it." He was afraid, and said, "How awesome this place is! This is none other than God's house, and this is the gate of heaven."

Jacob rose up early in the morning and took the stone that he had put under his head, and set it up for a pillar, and poured oil on its top. He called the name of that place Bethel, but the name of the city was Luz at the first. Jacob vowed a vow, saying, "If God will be with me, and will keep me in this way that I go, and will give me bread to eat, and clothing to put on, so that I come again to my father's house in peace, and Yahweh will be my God, then this stone, which I have set up for a pillar, will be God's house. Of all that you will give me I will surely give a tenth to you." (Genesis 28:10–22 WEB)

FOUR WINDS

FOUR WINDS BY KAREN PARKER

The Greek word, Ἄνεμοι (*Anemose*) means "winds" or "spirit." Angels are spirits created by God to do His work. There are four higher-ranked angels known as Archangels. They are messengers and security guards around the four corners of the Earth. Uriel in the North, Michael in the South, Raphael in the East, and Gabriel in the West.

> In speaking of the angels he says, "He makes his angels spirits, and his servants flames of fire." (Hebrews 1:7 NIV)

> Regarding angels he says, The messengers are winds, the servants are tongues of fire. (Hebrews 1:7 MSG)

Sometimes in the Bible, "four winds" refers to extraordinary events.

> Daniel spoke and said, "I saw in my vision by night, and, behold, the four winds of the sky broke out on the great sea." (Daniel 7:2 WEB)

> Then he said to me, "Prophesy to the wind, prophesy, son of man, and tell the wind, 'The Lord Yahweh says: "Come from the four winds, breath, and breathe on these slain, that they may live."'" (Ezekiel 37:9 WEB)

Other times, Scripture will refer to the four winds in the tribulations of the end of times events.

"Immediately after the tribulation of those days the sun will be darkened, and the moon will not give its light; the stars will fall from heaven, and the powers of the heavens will be shaken. Then the sign of the Son of Man will appear in heaven, and then all the tribes of the earth will mourn, and they will see the Son of Man coming on the clouds of heaven with power and great glory. And He will send His angels with a great sound of a trumpet, and they will gather together His elect from the four winds, from one end of heaven to the other." (Matthew 24:29–31 NKJV)

There are seven major archangels—each presides over a day of the week and have a significant ray of colored light and possess their own virtue: Jophiel, Sunday, yellow, wisdom and beauty; Chamuel, Monday, rose pink, love; Michael, Tuesday, royal blue or orange, will; Raphael, Wednesday, green or yellow, healing; Uriel, Thursday, red gold, peace and wisdom; Gabriel, Friday, silver or white, purity and revelations; Zadkiel, Saturday, violet, freedom and mercy.

To clarify the light rays in these angels, it is a metaphysical system. When the angel color vibrates electromagnetic energy frequencies in the universe, it attracts angels with similar frequencies so they can work together. It is a form of communicating.

While these four winds, or archangels, are busy with God's orders, rest assured that from all four corners of the world, they are looking out for you, the elect—the Christians who study scripture, understand it, and know the signs of the end of times. Jesus says to have peace of mind and know that you will be saved.

So you also, when you see all these things, know that it is near—at the doors! (Matthew 24:33 NKJV)

May the peace of the Lord be with you always. Amen.

ARCHANGEL MICHAEL

Archangels are the highest-ranking angels in heaven. The word *arch* in Greek is *arche*, and it means "ruler"; and *angelos* is messenger. God assigns them the most important responsibilities in the heavenlies and here on Earth.

Archangel Michael is God's top-ranking angel; he leads all the other angels. Each archangel's name has a meaning: for instance, *Michael* means "Who is like God." He is also known as Saint Michael because with his strength and courage, he protects and defends God's people against evil and empowers believers to set their faith on fire for God. As a leader, he wields a sword, armor and a banner with enormous influence and power. His angelic color is blue, he is a seraphim angel, and he is in charge of the southern hemisphere.

> But Michael, the archangel, when contending with the devil and arguing about the body of Moses, dared not bring against him an abusive condemnation, but said, "May the Lord rebuke you!" (Jude 1:9 WEB)

The prayer to Saint Michael the Archangel:

> "Saint Michael the Archangel, defend us in battle. Be our protection against the wickedness

and snares of the devil. May God rebuke him, we humbly pray; and do thou, O Prince of the heavenly host, by the power of God, cast into hell Satan and all the evil spirits, who prowl through the world seeking the ruin of souls. Amen."

Saint Michael will accompany Jesus when He returns and will also escort the souls of God's people to heaven in the end times.

For the Lord himself will descend from heaven with a shout, with the voice of the archangel and with God's trumpet. The dead in Christ will rise first. (1 Thessalonians 4:16 WEB)

"At that time Michael will stand up, the great prince who stands for the children of your people; and there will be a time of trouble, such as never was since there was a nation even to that same time. At that time your people will be delivered, everyone who is found written in the book." (Daniel 12:1 WEB)

When the time comes for that great battle between good and evil is here, Saint Michael will lead an army of angels to defeat Satan and his demons for a final victory, then the unbelievers will be sent to hell. My spiritual director, Sister Regina, said, "People don't go to hell because of their sins. People go to hell for their unbelief."

There was war in the sky. Michael and his angels made war on the dragon. The dragon and his angels made war. They didn't prevail. No place was found for them any more in heaven. The great dragon was thrown down, the old serpent, he who is called the devil and Satan, the deceiver of the whole world. He was thrown down to the earth, and his angels were thrown down with him. I heard a loud voice in heaven, saying, "Now the salvation, the power, and the Kingdom of our God, and the authority of his Christ has come; for the accuser of our brothers has been thrown down, who accuses them before our God day and night. They overcame him because of the Lamb's blood, and because of the word of their testimony. They didn't love their life, even to death. Therefore rejoice, heavens, and you who dwell in them. Woe to the earth and to the sea, because the devil has gone down to you, having great wrath, knowing that he has but a short time." (Revelation 12:7–12 WEB)

So if you are searching for some truth, strength, and courage, Archangel Michael will support you, defend you in battle against Satan, and show you God's purpose for your life. Amen.

ARCHANGEL RAPHAEL

Archangel Raphael is the angel of healing. *Raphael* in Hebrew means "God heals." He has compassion for people who are physically, emotionally, and spiritually troubled. When he heals them, they feel God's peace and joy, and thus brings them closer to God. Raphael carries a staff, the Hippocratic oath staff, like the one that Moses used in the dessert to save the people from dying from snake bites. His color is green, and he oversees the eastern hemisphere.

In old Jewish text, Raphael is appointed to heal the earth of its evil and affliction and the maladies of mankind. In the Book of Enoch, God gives Raphael an assignment: "Restore the earth which the fallen angels have corrupted; and announce life to it, that I may revive it."

The Book of Tobit in the Catholic Bible, Raphael journeys with a boy, Tobias, bringing him safely home; and along the way, Raphael heals many. When they reach home, Raphael heals Tobias's blind father and drives out demons from Sarah. Tobias's father wants to repay him as a thank you, but Raphael only asks that they give praises to God.

"And because you were acceptable to God,
it was necessary for you to be tested by trials. And
now, the Lord has sent me to cure you, and to

free Sarah, your son's wife, from the demon. For I am the Angel Raphael, one of seven, who stand before the Lord." And when they had heard these things, they were troubled, and being seized with fear, they fell upon the ground on their face. And the Angel said to them: "Peace be to you. Fear not. For when I was with you, I was there by the will of God. Bless him and sing to him. Indeed, I seemed to eat and drink with you, but I make use of an invisible food and drink, which cannot be seen by men. Therefore, it is time that I return to him who sent me. But as for you, bless God, and describe all his wonders." And when he had said these things, he was taken from their sight, and they were not able to see him any longer. Then, lying prostrate for three hours upon their face, they blessed God. And rising up, they described all his wonders. (Tobit 12:13–22 CPDV)

ARCHANGEL GABRIEL

Archangel Gabriel is known as the angel to reveal a revelation of God's. His color is white. He is depicted with symbols of blowing a horn, holding a shield, a staff, a lantern, and sometimes an olive branch. When Christ returns in His second coming, it will be Gabriel blowing his horn loud like thunder and awaken the dead on judgment day. In Hebrew, Gabriel's name means "hero of God" and "God is my strength."

Archangel Gabriel was the angel that God sent to deliver the greatest messages of all. He was chosen to announce that God Himself was to come and bring salvation to His people. Jesus, a savior, will bring us eternal life.

He first appeared to Zechariah, a high priest, telling him that his barren wife was going to have a child and that this child was to be called John. John the Baptist would prepare people and make way for the coming Messiah.

> An angel of the Lord appeared to him, standing on the right side of the altar of incense. Zacharias was troubled when he saw him, and fear fell upon him. But the angel said to him, "Don't be afraid, Zacharias, because your request has been heard. Your wife, Elizabeth, will bear you a son, and you shall call his name John. You

will have joy and gladness, and many will rejoice at his birth. For he will be great in the sight of the Lord, and he will drink no wine nor strong drink. He will be filled with the Holy Spirit, even from his mother's womb. He will turn many of the children of Israel to the Lord their God. He will go before him in the spirit and power of Elijah, 'to turn the hearts of the fathers to the children, and the disobedient to the wisdom of the just; to prepare a people prepared for the Lord.'" (Luke 1:11–17 WEB) (See reference: Malachi 4:6)

The angel answered him, "I am Gabriel, who stands in the presence of God. I was sent to speak to you and to bring you this good news." (Luke 1:19 WEB)

Gabriel announced to the Virgin Mary that she would conceive a child of God and name Him Jesus. *Jesus* means "to deliver." *Immanuel* means "God is with us." *Messiah* means "anointed one."

Now in the sixth month, the angel Gabriel was sent from God to a city of Galilee named Nazareth, to a virgin pledged to be married to a man whose name was Joseph, of David's house. The virgin's name was Mary. Having come in, the angel said to her, "Rejoice, you highly favored one! The Lord is with you. Blessed are you among women!"

But when she saw him, she was greatly troubled at the saying, and considered what kind of salutation this might be. The angel said to her, "Don't be afraid, Mary, for you have found favor with God. Behold, you will conceive in your womb and give birth to a son, and shall name him 'Jesus.' He will be great and will be called the

Son of the Most High. The Lord God will give him the throne of his father David, and he will reign over the house of Jacob forever. There will be no end to his Kingdom."

Mary said to the angel, "How can this be, seeing I am a virgin?"

The angel answered her, "The Holy Spirit will come on you, and the power of the Most High will overshadow you. Therefore, also the holy one who is born from you will be called the Son of God. Behold, Elizabeth your relative also has conceived a son in her old age; and this is the sixth month with her who was called barren. For nothing spoken by God is impossible."

Mary said, "Behold, the servant of the Lord; let it be done to me according to your word." (Luke 1:26–38 WEB)

Mary and Joseph were in Bethlehem, and Mary was about to give birth to Jesus. Gabriel came down from heaven, along with the whole army of God's heavenly angels, to announce to the shepherds in the fields nearby that their savior is born. This is truly the most joyous and greatest message of all times.

While they were there, the day had come for her to give birth. She gave birth to her firstborn son. She wrapped him in bands of cloth, and laid him in a feeding trough, because there was no room for them in the inn. There were shepherds in the same country staying in the field and keeping watch by night over their flock. Behold, an angel of the Lord stood by them, and the glory of the Lord shone around them, and they were terrified. The angel said to them, "Don't be afraid, for behold, I bring you good news of great joy which will be to all the people. For there is born to you today, in David's city, a Savior, who is Christ the Lord. This is the sign to you: you will find a baby wrapped in strips of cloth, lying in a feeding trough." Suddenly, there was with the angel a multitude of the heavenly army praising God, and saying,

"Glory to God in the highest, on earth peace, good will toward men."

When the angels went away from them into the sky, the shepherds said to one another, "Let's go to Bethlehem, now, and see this thing that has happened, which the Lord has made known to us." They came with haste, and found both Mary and Joseph, and the baby was lying in the feeding trough. When they saw it, they publicized widely the saying which was spoken to them about this child. All who heard it wondered at the things which were spoken to them by the shepherds. But Mary kept all these sayings, pondering them in her heart. The shepherds returned, glorifying and praising God for all the things that they had heard and seen, just as it was told them. (Luke 2:6–20 WEB)

The prophet Daniel was praying to God, asking to save His people, and Gabriel came to give Daniel insight and understanding.

"Now therefore, our God, listen to the prayer of your servant, and to his petitions, and cause your face to shine on your sanctuary that is desolate, for the Lord's sake. My God, turn your ear, and hear. Open your eyes, and see our desolations, and the city which is called by your name; for we do not present our petitions before you for our righteousness, but for your great mercies' sake. Lord, hear. Lord, forgive. Lord, listen and do. Don't defer, for your own sake, my God, because your city and your people are called by your name."

While I was speaking, praying, and confessing my sin and the sin of my people Israel, and presenting my supplication before Yahweh my God for the holy mountain of my God; yes, while I was speaking in prayer, the man Gabriel, whom I had seen in the vision at the beginning, being caused to fly swiftly, touched me about the time of the evening offering. He instructed me and talked with me, and said, "Daniel, I have now come to give you wisdom and understanding. At the beginning of your petitions the commandment went out, and I have come to tell you; for you are greatly beloved. Therefore, consider the matter, and understand the vision. (Daniel 9:17–23 WEB)

"Seventy weeks are decreed on your people and on your holy city, to finish disobedience, and to make an end of sins, and to make reconciliation for iniquity, and to bring in everlasting righteousness, and to seal up vision and prophecy, and to anoint the most holy.

"Know therefore and discern that from the going out of the commandment to restore and to build Jerusalem to the Anointed One, the prince, will be seven weeks and sixty-two weeks." (Daniel 9:24–25 WEB)

ARCHANGEL URIEL

"Love is my destiny; you are my fate."

—Anonymous

Archangel Uriel is the angel known for wisdom. His name means "God is my light." Uriel is the angel of the north. His color is red. He shines God's light of truth into the dark, bringing wisdom and understanding to confusion and chaos. He helps us solve problems, let go of anxiety and anger, and how to recognize and avoid dangerous situations. He is shown representing a book, a scroll, and holding a flame of fire that is God's truth.

> In all their affliction he was afflicted, and the angel of his presence saved them. In his love and in his pity, he redeemed them. He bore them and carried them all the days of old. (Isaiah 63:9 WEB)

Enoch was Seth's fifth generation who walked faithfully with God. Seth was Adam and Eve's third son who became a pre-patriarch father of generations to come; he was the first of Jesus's descendants.

Enoch walked faithfully with God; then he was no more, because God took him away. (Genesis 5:24 NIV)

Enoch was a righteous man, blameless in God's eye. He was one of the only two men mentioned in the Bible whom God had taken up by angels to heaven, escaping death. The other man was the prophet Elijah. The Books of Enoch were rejected by the Jewish people from being placed in the Old Testament canon because it contained prophecies pertaining to Jesus Christ. Enoch, after all, was a descendant of Jesus, and now that we know Enoch's prophesies were true and correct, we should consider his writings to be from God.

Uriel came to warn Noah about the upcoming flood in the Book of Enoch.

Then said the Most High, the Holy and Great One spake, and sent Uriel to the son of Lamech, and said to him: "Go to Noah and tell him in my name. Hide thyself!" and reveal to him the end that is approaching: that the whole earth will be destroyed, and a deluge is about to come upon the whole earth and will destroy all that is on it. And now instruct him that he may escape, and his seed may be preserved for all the generations of the world.' (The Book of Enoch 10:1–4)

Uriel is recognized as the patron saint of the sacrament of confirmation. In many Jewish writings, Uriel was the angel who rescued John the Baptist from Herod's massacre and was the angel who buried Adam and Abel in the garden of Eden. Uriel was the angel who led Abraham's people to Canaan. He was responsible for insuring everyone's faith to God during the Passover by checking for the lamb's blood over the doors during the plague in Egypt. Uriel also holds the key to the pit of hell during the end of days. When Adam and Eve were banished from paradise, he is the angel that held the fiery sword and stood beside the cherubim guarding the gates of Eden.

> So, he drove out the man; and he placed cherubim at the east of the garden of Eden, and a flaming sword which turned every way, to guard the way to the tree of life. (Genesis 3:24 WEB)

ARCHANGEL PHANUEL

Archangel Phanuel, also known as Peniel, was the man who wrestled with Jacob. *Phanuel* means "the face of God." This is the angel of hope and repentance. Encouraging people to repent their sins and overcome guilt and regret, they can pursue a life of right relationship with God.

In the story, Jacob was on his way to visit with his brother Esau in hopes that they could reconcile their differences. As he approached the riverbanks, a mysterious man came and began to struggle with Jacob. This man was Archangel Phanuel. After Jacob wrestled with Peniel, he meets his brother Esau and learned he had forgiven him.

> But Esau ran to meet him, and embraced him, and fell on his neck and kissed him, and they wept. (Genesis 33:4 NKJV)

Here is the story where Jacob wrestles with God and his name changes to Israel:

> Jacob was left alone and wrestled with a man there until the breaking of the day. When he saw that he didn't prevail against him, the man touched the hollow of his thigh, and the hollow

of Jacob's thigh was strained as he wrestled. The man said, "Let me go, for the day breaks."

Jacob said, "I won't let you go unless you bless me."

He said to him, "What is your name?"

He said, "Jacob".

He said, "Your name will no longer be called Jacob, but Israel; for you have fought with God and with men, and have prevailed."

Jacob asked him, "Please tell me your name."

He said, "Why is it that you ask what my name is?" So he blessed him there.

Jacob called the name of the place Peniel; for he said, "I have seen God face to face, and my life is preserved." The sun rose on him as he passed over Peniel, and he limped because of his thigh. Therefore the children of Israel don't eat the sinew of the hip, which is on the hollow of the thigh, to this day, because he touched the hollow of Jacob's thigh in the sinew of the hip. (Genesis 32:24–32 WEB)

The Hebrew meaning and the Bible refers the name *Israel* as "who wrestles with God." All of humanity are Israelites because we all, from time to time, wrestle with God. Sometimes it is in this wrestling that we struggle to understand why God allows us to suffer. It is in God's nature for us to experience life's struggles for us to strengthen our faith. The Archangel Phanuel will help us to understand our own hope and repentance.

ARCHANGEL SELAPHIEL

Archangel Selaphiel is the angel of prayer. His name means "the prayer of God." He helps people to pray earnestly to God and to express their true feelings. Prayer connects us directly to God, and God will answer us through prayer; we just have to take the time to listen to His voice. Selaphiel is depicted in Catholic art as holding a golden censer that holds the smoke of burning incense that are the prayers of the saints. He is also the patron saint of prayers.

In Revelation, Selaphiel prepares to give God a golden censer full of prayers of the saints and then threw them to Earth. Seven other angels prepare for seven plagues from God to fall upon the earth. And then finally, Wormwood was destroyed, fell to earth, and brought bitterness to the waters.

> When he opened the seventh seal, there was silence in heaven for about half an hour. I saw the seven angels who stand before God, and seven trumpets were given to them.
>
> Another angel came and stood over the altar, having a golden censer. Much incense was given to him, that he should add it to the prayers of all the saints on the golden altar which was before the throne. The smoke of the incense, with the

prayers of the saints, went up before God out of the angel's hand. The angel took the censer, and he filled it with the fire of the altar, then threw it on the earth. Thunders, sounds, lightnings, and an earthquake followed.

The seven angels who had the seven trumpets prepared themselves to sound. The first sounded, and there followed hail and fire, mixed with blood, and they were thrown to the earth. One third of the earth was burned up, and one third of the trees were burned up, and all green grass was burned up.

The second angel sounded, and something like a great burning mountain was thrown into the sea. One third of the sea became blood, and one third of the living creatures which were in the sea died. One third of the ships were destroyed.

The third angel sounded, and a great star fell from the sky, burning like a torch, and it fell on one third of the rivers, and on the springs of the waters. The name of the star is called "Wormwood." One third of the waters became wormwood. Many people died from the waters, because they were made bitter.

The fourth angel sounded, and one third of the sun was struck, and one third of the moon, and one third of the stars; so that one third of them would be darkened, and the day wouldn't shine for one third of it, and the night in the same way. I saw, and I heard an eagle, flying in mid heaven, saying with a loud voice, "Woe! Woe! Woe for those who dwell on the earth, because of the other voices of the trumpets of the three angels, who are yet to sound!" (Revelation 8:1–13 WEB)

The fifth angel sounded, and I saw a star from the sky which had fallen to the earth. The key to the pit of the abyss was given to him. He opened the pit of the abyss, and smoke went up out of the pit, like the smoke from a burning furnace. The sun and the air were darkened because of the smoke from the pit. Then out of the smoke came locusts on the earth, and power was given to them, as the scorpions of the earth have power. They were told that they should not hurt the grass of the earth, neither any green thing, neither any tree, but only those people who don't have God's seal on their foreheads. (Revelation 9:1–4 WEB)

The sixth angel sounded. I heard a voice from the horns of the golden altar, which is before God, saying to the sixth angel who had the trumpet, "Free the four angels who are bound at the great river Euphrates!" (Revelation 9:13–14 WEB)

Now before the angels were allowed to deliver the plagues, God told them to no harm anyone until they have sealed the servants of our God on their foreheads. The four angels standing at the four corners of the earth were the Archangels: Saint Uriel of the north, Saint Michael of the south, Saint Raphael of the east, and Saint Gabriel of the west. All those who are written in the book of life shall be spared the tribulation.

After this, I saw four angels standing at the four corners of the earth, holding the four winds of the earth, so that no wind would blow on the earth, or on the sea, or on any tree. I saw another angel ascend from the sunrise, having the seal of the living God. He cried with a loud voice to the four angels to whom it was given to harm the earth and the sea, saying, "Don't harm the earth, the sea, or the trees, until we have sealed the bondservants of our God on their foreheads!" I heard the number of those who were sealed, one hundred forty-four thousand, sealed out of every tribe of the children of Israel:

of the tribe of Judah twelve thousand were sealed,

of the tribe of Reuben twelve thousand,

of the tribe of Gad twelve thousand,

of the tribe of Asher twelve thousand,

of the tribe of Naphtali twelve thousand,

of the tribe of Manasseh twelve thousand,

of the tribe of Simeon twelve thousand,

of the tribe of Levi twelve thousand,

of the tribe of Issachar twelve thousand,

of the tribe of Zebulun twelve thousand,

of the tribe of Joseph twelve thousand, and

of the tribe of Benjamin twelve thousand were sealed. (Revelation 7:1–8 WEB)

ARCHANGEL UZZIEL

Archangel Uzziel is the angel of faith. *Uzziel* in Hebrew means "strength of God." He helps people accelerate and grow in their faith. True faith is found deep inside your soul, and this is something that our forefathers, the patriarch, had. The Old Testament is filled with stories of people who were embraced with great faith, and it is that faith that obtains a good testimony for God. Faith inspires a right action and can work miracles beyond the human understanding. It was faith that called Abraham to lead his people, it was with faith that Joseph saved all of Egypt and the Israelites, it was by faith that Moses took his people through the wilderness to the promised land, and it was by faith that Jesus was crucified for our salvation. Faith is the substance of things hoped for, the evidence of things not seen. The CCC (Catechism of the Catholic Church) reads in paragraph 328, "The existence of the spiritual, non-corporeal beings that sacred Scripture usually calls *angels*, is a truth of faith. The witness of Scripture is as clear as the unanimity of Tradition."

The Apostle Paul says it perfectly:

> Now faith is assurance of things hoped for, proof of things not seen. For by this, the elders obtained testimony. By faith, we understand that the universe has been framed by the word of God, so that what is seen has not been made out of things which are visible.

By faith, Abel offered to God a more excellent sacrifice than Cain, through which he had testimony given to him that he was righteous, God testifying with respect to his gifts; and through it he, being dead, still speaks. By faith, Enoch was taken away, so that he wouldn't see death, and he was not found, because God translated him. For he has had testimony given to him that before his translation he had been well pleasing to God. Without faith it is impossible to be well pleasing to him, for he who comes to God must believe that he exists, and that he is a rewarder of those who seek him.

By faith, Noah, being warned about things not yet seen, moved with godly fear, prepared a ship for the saving of his house, through which he condemned the world, and became heir of the righteousness which is according to faith. By faith, Abraham, when he was called, obeyed to go out to the place which he was to receive for an inheritance. He went out, not knowing where he went. By faith, he lived as an alien in the land of promise, as in a land not his own, dwelling in tents with Isaac and Jacob, the heirs with him of the same promise. For he looked for the city which has the foundations, whose builder and maker is God.

By faith, even Sarah herself received power to conceive, and she bore a child when she was past age, since she counted him faithful who had promised. Therefore as many as the stars of the sky in multitude, and as innumerable as the sand which is by the sea shore, were fathered by one man, and him as good as dead.

These all died in faith, not having received the promises, but having seen them and embraced them from afar, and having confessed that they were strangers and pilgrims on the earth. For those who say such things make it clear that they are seeking a country of their own. If indeed they had been thinking of that country from which they went out, they would have had enough time to return. But now they desire a better country, that is, a heavenly one. Therefore, God is not ashamed of them, to be called their God, for he has prepared a city for them.

By faith, Abraham, being tested, offered up Isaac. Yes, he who had gladly received the promises was offering up his one and only son, to whom it was said, "Your offspring will be accounted as from Isaac," concluding that God is able to raise up even from the dead. Figuratively speaking, he also did receive him back from the dead.

By faith, Isaac blessed Jacob and Esau, even concerning things to come.

By faith, Jacob, when he was dying, blessed each of the sons of Joseph, and worshiped, leaning on the top of his staff.

By faith, Joseph, when his end was near, made mention of the departure of the children of Israel, and gave instructions concerning his bones.

By faith, Moses, when he was born, was hidden for three months by his parents, because they saw that he was a beautiful child, and they were not afraid of the king's commandment.

By faith, Moses, when he had grown up, refused to be called the son of Pharaoh's daughter, choosing rather to share ill treatment with God's people than to enjoy the pleasures of sin for a time, considering the reproach of Christ greater riches than the treasures of Egypt; for he looked to the reward. By faith, he left Egypt, not fearing the wrath of the king; for he endured, as seeing him who is invisible. By faith, he kept the Passover, and the sprinkling of the blood, that the destroyer of the firstborn should not touch them. By faith, they passed through the Red Sea as on dry land. When the Egyptians tried to do so, they were swallowed up. By faith, the walls of Jericho fell down, after they had been encircled for seven days.

By faith, Rahab the prostitute didn't perish with those who were disobedient, having received the spies in peace.

What more shall I say? For the time would fail me if I told of Gideon, Barak, Samson, Jephthah, David, Samuel, and the prophets, who through faith subdued kingdoms, worked out righteousness, obtained promises, stopped the mouths of lions, quenched the power of fire, escaped the edge of the sword, from weakness were made strong, grew mighty in war, and caused foreign armies to flee. Women received their dead by resurrection. Others were tortured, not accepting their deliverance, that they might obtain a better resurrection. Others were tried by mocking and scourging, yes, moreover by bonds and imprisonment. They were stoned. They were sawn apart. They were tempted. They were slain with the sword. They went around in sheep skins and in goat skins; being destitute, afflicted, ill-treated—of whom the world was not worthy—wandering in deserts, mountains, caves, and the holes of the earth.

These all, having had testimony given to them through their faith, didn't receive the promise, God having provided some better thing concerning us, so that apart from us they should not be made perfect. (Hebrews 11:1–40 WEB) (See references: Genesis 21:12; Daniel 6:22–23; Daniel 3:1–30; 1 Kings 19:1–3; 2 Kings 6:31–7:20; 1 Kings 17:17–23; 2 Kings 4:32–37; 2 Chronicles 24:20–21; Jeremiah 26:20–23; 1 Kings 19:10)

Therefore let's also, seeing we are surrounded by so great a cloud of witnesses, lay aside every weight and the sin which so easily entangles us, and let's run with perseverance the race that is set before us, looking to Jesus, the author and perfecter of faith, who for the joy that was set before him endured the cross, despising its shame, and has sat down at the right hand of the throne of God. (Hebrews 12:1–2 WEB)

Archangel Uzziel surely manifested the strength of God to each one of these courageous people. Through their faith alone, they moved mountains, divided the sea, conquered kingdoms, and made the angels cry. They showed us what the powers of true faith brings and changed the world as we know it.

May your faith in God bring you peace and joy. In Jesus's name, I pray. Amen.

ARCHANGEL JOPHIEL

Archangel Jophiel is the angel known for beauty. In Hebrew, her name means "beauty of God." As we think of beautiful thoughts, we develop a beautiful soul. As we begin to understand God's beauty in all His creation, we begin to understand His love for us and recognize how valuable we are to Him.

The three wise men were to have followed the star of Bethlehem for years, looking for a new king to worship. A king who will bring good tidings of great joy to all. With the help of an angel, they succeeded to find baby Jesus in a manger the day he was born. The three wise men were three astronomers, alchemists, and kings known as Balthasar, king of Arabia; Melchior, king of Persia; and Gaspar, king of India. The three gifts that they brought to Jesus had spiritual meaning. The gold is a symbol for kings because only kings could possess it; frankincense is a symbol of deity. It is incense that is burned with an offering of prayer to God, and myrrh was an oil used on the dead as a symbol of one who was mortal.

> Now when Jesus was born in Bethlehem of Judaea in the days of Herod the king, behold, Wise-men from the east came to Jerusalem, saying, Where is he that is born King of the Jews? for we saw his star in the east, and are come to worship him. And when Herod the king heard it, he was troubled, and all Jerusalem with him. And gathering together all the chief priests and

scribes of the people, he inquired of them where the Christ should be born. And they said unto him, In Bethlehem of Judaea: for thus it is written through the prophet,

And thou Bethlehem, land of Judah,

Art in no wise least among the princes of Judah:

For out of thee shall come forth a governor,

Who shall be shepherd of my people Israel.

Then Herod privately called the Wise-men, and learned of them exactly what time the star appeared. And he sent them to Bethlehem, and said, Go and search out exactly concerning the young child; and when ye have found *him*, bring me word, that I also may come and worship him. And they, having heard the king, went their way; and lo, the star, which they saw in the east, went before them, till it came and stood over where the young child was. And when they saw the star, they rejoiced with exceeding great joy. And they came into the house and saw the young child with Mary his mother; and they fell down and worshipped him; and opening their treasures they offered unto him gifts, gold and frankincense and myrrh. And being warned of God in a dream that they should not return to Herod, they departed into their own country another way.

Now when they were departed, behold, an angel of the Lord appeareth to Joseph in a dream, saying, Arise and take the young child and his mother, and flee into Egypt, and be thou there until I tell thee: for Herod will seek the young child to destroy him. (Matthew 2:1–13 ASV)

ARCHANGEL ZADKIEL

Zadkiel is the angel of mercy. His name means "righteousness of God." He is often depicted as holding a dagger. Zadkiel helps people who need God's mercy, whether it be of mercy through a sin that they are working out, or when they need God's mercy for something unjust that has been placed upon them. Through faith in God, Zadkiel will encourage people that God cares and will be merciful to them.

> Then they came to the place of which God had told him. And Abraham built an altar there and placed the wood in order; and he bound Isaac his son and laid him on the altar, upon the wood. And Abraham stretched out his hand and took the knife to slay his son.
>
> But the Angel of the LORD called to him from heaven and said, "Abraham, Abraham!"
>
> So he said, "Here I am."
>
> And He said, "Do not lay your hand on the lad, or do anything to him; for now I know that you fear God, since you have not withheld your son, your only *son*, from Me." (Genesis 22:9–12 NKJV)

Then the king arose very early in the morning and went in haste to the den of lions. When he came near to the den to Daniel, he cried with a troubled voice. The king spoke and said to Daniel, "Daniel, servant of the living God, is your God, whom you serve continually, able to deliver you from the lions?"

Then Daniel said to the king, "O king, live forever! My God has sent his angel, and has shut the lions' mouths, and they have not hurt me; because as before him innocence was found in me; and also before you, O king, I have done no harm." (Daniel 6:19–22 WEB)

Shadrach, Meshach, and Abednego answered the king, "Nebuchadnezzar, we have no need to answer you in this matter. If it happens, our God whom we serve is able to deliver us from the burning fiery furnace; and he will deliver us out of your hand, O king. But if not, let it be known to you, O king, that we will not serve your gods or worship the golden image which you have set up." (Daniel 3:16–18 WEB)

One of the famous miracles in the Bible is of Shadrach, Meshach, and Abednego. King Nebuchadnezzar was punishing them for not kneeling down and worshiping his statue. These three men were righteous and only praised the God of Abraham, Isaac, and Jacob. They were rescued by an angel of God from a fiery blazing furnace.

Then Nebuchadnezzar was full of fury, and the form of his appearance was changed against Shadrach, Meshach, and Abednego. He spoke, and commanded that they should heat the furnace seven times more than it was usually heated. He commanded certain mighty men who were in his army to bind Shadrach, Meshach, and Abednego, and to cast them into the burning fiery furnace. Then these men were bound in their pants, their tunics, and their mantles, and their other clothes, and were cast into the middle of the burning fiery furnace. Therefore because the king's commandment was urgent, and the furnace exceedingly hot, the flame of the fire killed those men who took up Shadrach, Meshach, and Abednego. These three men, Shadrach, Meshach, and Abednego fell down bound into the middle of the burning fiery furnace.

Then Nebuchadnezzar the king was astonished and rose up in haste. He spoke and said to his counselors, "Didn't we cast three men bound into the middle of the fire?"

They answered the king, "True, O king."

He answered, "Look, I see four men loose, walking in the middle of the fire, and they are unharmed. The appearance of the fourth is like a son of the gods."

Then Nebuchadnezzar came near to the mouth of the burning fiery furnace. He spoke and said, "Shadrach, Meshach, and Abednego, you servants of the Most High God, come out, and come here!"

Then Shadrach, Meshach, and Abednego came out of the middle of the fire. The local governors, the deputies, and the governors, and the king's counselors, being gathered together, saw these men, that the fire had no power on their bodies. The hair of their head wasn't singed. Their pants weren't changed, the smell of fire wasn't even on them.

Nebuchadnezzar spoke and said, "Blessed be the God of Shadrach, Meshach, and Abednego, who has sent his angel and delivered his servants who trusted in him, and have changed the king's word, and have yielded their bodies, that they might not serve nor worship any god, except their own God." (Daniel 3:19–28 WEB)

One of my favorite stories is the talking donkey. A sorcerer named Balaam was sent by King Balak to curse the Israelites and to bring evil upon the Hebrew people, but instead God's angel made Balaam put a blessing on the Israelites instead of a curse.

"Balaam rose up in the morning, and saddled his donkey, and went with the princes of Moab. God's anger burned because he went; and Yahweh's angel placed himself in the way as an adversary against him. Now he was riding on his donkey, and his two servants were with him. The donkey saw Yahweh's angel standing in the way, with his sword drawn in his hand; and the donkey turned out of the path and went into the field. Balaam struck the donkey, to turn her into the path. Then Yahweh's angel stood in a narrow path between the vineyards, a wall being on this side, and a wall on that side. The donkey saw Yahweh's angel, and she thrust herself to the wall, and crushed Balaam's foot against the wall. He struck her again.

Yahweh's angel went further, and stood in a narrow place, where there was no way to turn either to the right hand or to the left. The donkey saw Yahweh's angel, and she lay down under Balaam. Balaam's anger burned, and he struck the donkey with his staff.

Yahweh opened the mouth of the donkey, and she said to Balaam, "What have I done to you, that you have struck me these three times?"

Balaam said to the donkey, "Because you have mocked me, I wish there were a sword in my hand, for now I would have killed you."

The donkey said to Balaam, "Am I not your donkey, on which you have ridden all your life long until today? Was I ever in the habit of doing so to you?"

He said, "No."

Then Yahweh opened the eyes of Balaam, and he saw Yahweh's angel standing in the way, with his sword drawn in his hand; and he bowed his head and fell on his face. Yahweh's angel said to him, "Why have you struck your donkey these three times? Behold, I have come out as an adversary, because your way is perverse before me. The donkey saw me, and turned away before me these three times. Unless she had turned away from me, surely now I would have killed you, and saved her alive."

Balaam said to Yahweh's angel, "I have sinned; for I didn't know that you stood in the way against me. Now therefore, if it displeases you, I will go back again." Yahweh's angel said to Balaam, "Go with the men; but you shall only speak the word that I shall speak to you." (Numbers 22:21–35 WEB)

ARCHANGEL CHAMUEL

Chamuel is the angel of peaceful relationships. His name in Hebrew means "one who seeks God." He is depicted with a heart on his chest, and his color is pink. He represents love and helps people find inner peace, restores relationships, and offers healing when under great stress.

One such time was when Jesus went to the garden of Gethsemane to pray to His Father. As He began to pray, He suddenly felt the weight of suffering for our sins. This is when His suffering would begin for the crucifixion. His soul began to feel very troubled and deeply distressed.

> "My soul is exceedingly sorrowful, *even* to death." (Mark 14:34 NKJV)

The word *Gethsemane* in Greek means "crushed," like grapes being crushed in a grape press. Jesus prayed to His Father to not have this terrible thing happen to Him, but His Father sent Him for this very reason: to die for our sins, to be crushed for our iniquities, and to bear the full weight and burden of our sins.

Jesus's agonizing prayer in the garden of Gethsemane was because He could see visions of what was about to happen to Him in the betrayal, arrest, trial, beatings, mocking, scourging, carrying the cross, the final crucifixion on the cross, and then death. While He was praying, He sweat blood; this is a rare condition known as "hematohidrosis" which means that a person's, under the pressure of great stress, blood vessels constrict as the anxiety passes, and the blood vessels then dilate to the point of rupture. Sometimes a soldier will sweat blood before a battle.

> He came out and went, as his custom was, to the Mount of Olives. His disciples also followed him. When he was at the place, he said to them, "Pray that you don't enter into temptation."
>
> He was withdrawn from them about a stone's throw, and he knelt down and prayed, saying, "Father, if you are willing, remove this cup from me. Nevertheless, not my will, but yours, be done."
>
> An angel from heaven appeared to him, strengthening him.
>
> Being in agony he prayed more earnestly. His sweat became like great drops of blood falling down on the ground. (Luke 22:39–44 WEB)

ARCHANGEL METATRON

Archangel Metatron is the angel of life. His name means "one who guards" or "one serves behind God's throne." Some believe that Metatron can gaze on the countenance of God. He is a scribe for God, writing down the deeds of people, angels, and is a mediator between God and Israel. In art, he is depicted as the angel that guards the tree of life. His color: blue, green, and pink stripes.

> Yahweh God said, "Behold, the man has become like one of us, knowing good and evil. Now, lest he reach out his hand, and also take of the tree of life, and eat, and live forever—" Therefore Yahweh God sent him out from the garden of Eden, to till the ground from which he was taken. So he drove out the man; and he placed cherubim at the east of the garden of Eden, and a flaming sword which turned every way, to guard the way to the tree of life. (Genesis 3:22–24 WEB)

In the Zohar, the holy book of Judaism, Metatron was once the human prophet Enoch, whom God took to heaven. Then Enoch was transformed into an angel. When God took him, he was writing a book on the inner secrets of wisdom.

In the Talmud, another Jewish holy book, it says that "Metatron, to whom was given permission to sit down and write the merits of Israel."

During the time of the Exodus, God sent an angel to travel through the wilderness with the Israelites.

"Behold, I send an angel before you, to keep you by the way, and to bring you into the place which I have prepared. Pay attention to him and listen to his voice. Don't provoke him, for he will not pardon your disobedience, for my name is in him. But if you indeed listen to his voice, and do all that I speak, then I will be an enemy to your enemies, and an adversary to your adversaries. For my angel shall go before you, and bring you in to the Amorite, the Hittite, the Perizzite, the Canaanite, the Hivite, and the Jebusite; and I will cut them off. You shall not bow down to their gods, nor serve them, nor follow their practices, but you shall utterly overthrow them and demolish their pillars. You shall serve Yahweh your God, and he will bless your bread and your water, and I will take sickness away from among you. No one will miscarry or be barren in your land. I will fulfill the number of your days." (Exodus 23:20–26 WEB)

NEPHILIM

When men began to multiply on the surface of the ground and daughters were born to them, God's sons saw that men's daughters were beautiful, and they took any that they wanted for themselves as wives. Yahweh said, "My Spirit will not strive with man forever, because he also is flesh; so, his days will be one hundred twenty years." The Nephilim were in the earth in those days, and also after that, when God's sons came in to men's daughters and had children with them. Those were the mighty men who were of old, men of renown.

Yahweh saw that the wickedness of man was great in the earth, and that every imagination of the thoughts of man's heart was continually only evil. (Genesis 6:1–5 WEB)

The word *Nephilim* in Hebrew is *naphal* and means "to fall" or "the fallen ones." The sons of God, or the angels that have fallen from heaven to Earth, married daughters of men, daughters of Cain; their offspring were called Nephilim's. These daughters of men were daughters of Cain's wicked line of descendants after the fall of man. These Nephilims are the offspring's of men of old and were giants in the days before the flood.

Now some theologians believe that the sons of God were sons of the righteous men of Adam's third child, Seth. But these men were righteous in the eyes of the Lord and would never lust or do something morally wrong because it is an abomination to the Lord. Cain's decedents were the only other people in those days. They were labeled vagabonds by God because of Cain killing his brother, Abel. God then gave Cain a mark and abandoned him from Eden.

> And Cain said to the Lord, "My punishment is greater than I can bear! Surely You have driven me out this day from the face of the ground; I shall be hidden from Your face; I shall be a fugitive and a vagabond on the earth, and it will happen that anyone who finds me will kill me.
> And the Lord said to him, "Therefore, whoever kills Cain, vengeance shall be taken on him sevenfold." And the Lord set a mark on Cain, lest anyone finding him should kill him."
> (Genesis 4:13–15 NKJV)

In the Book of Job is another scripture that reads the sons of God are the fallen angels.

> Now there was a day when the sons of God came to present themselves before the Lord, and Satan came also among them.
> And the Lord said unto Satan, Whence comest thou? Then Satan answered the Lord, and said, From going to and fro in the earth, and from walking up and down in it. (Job 1:6–7 KJV)

The comingling of Cain's descendants with these celestial beings or sons of God called forth the great flood.

> Yahweh was sorry that he had made man on the earth, and it grieved him in his heart.

Yahweh said, "I will destroy man whom I have created from the surface of the ground—man, along with animals, creeping things, and birds of the sky—for I am sorry that I have made them." But Noah found favor in Yahweh's eyes. (Genesis 6:6–8 WEB)

After the flood, a few giants appeared, and some theologians believe that Nephilim genes were passed down through Noah's daughters-in-law. Goliath and Og were giants as well as some Emites, Ammonites, and Rephaim. People were terrified of these giants, but they were also considered to be heroes and great warriors because of their strength and courage.

A cubit is about eighteen inches; King Og's bed was thirteen feet, six inches long.

(For only Og king of Bashan remained of the remnant of the Rephaim. Behold, his bedstead was a bedstead of iron. Isn't it in Rabbah of the children of Ammon? Nine cubits was its length, and four cubits its width, after the cubit of a man.) (Deuteronomy 3:11 WEB)

David did not just defeat a random giant; Goliath was almost ten feet tall and mighty in strength. His coat of armor weighed ninety-two pounds.

A champion out of the camp of the Philistines named Goliath of Gath, whose height was six cubits and a span went out. He had a helmet of bronze on his head, and he wore a coat of mail; and the weight of the coat was five thousand shekels of bronze. He had bronze shin armor on his legs and a bronze javelin between his shoulders. The staff of his spear was like a weaver's beam; and his spear's head weighed six hundred shekels of iron. His shield bearer went before him. (1 Samuel 17:4–7 WEB)

Here are a couple more scriptures on the Nephilim.

They will not lie with the mighty who are fallen of the uncircumcised, who have gone down to Sheol with their weapons of war, and have laid their swords under their heads, and their iniquities are on their bones; for they were the terror of the mighty in the land of the living. (Ezekiel 32:27 WEB)

But the men who went up with him said, "We aren't able to go up against the people; for they are stronger than we." They brought up an evil report of the land which they had spied out to the children of Israel, saying, "The land, through which we have gone to spy it out, is a land that eats up its inhabitants; and all the people who we saw in it are men of great stature. There we saw the Nephilim, the sons of Anak, who come from the Nephilim. We were in our own sight as grasshoppers, and so we were in their sight." (Numbers 13:31–33 WEB)

FALLEN ANGELS

Fallen angels are angels that have fallen from rank and fell from heaven to Earth. Fallen angels are Lucifer's minions. When God created angels, they were holy and pure and good. But when the most beautiful angel, Lucifer—also known as Satan—got jealous of God; he rebelled against Him, so God expelled Lucifer from heaven. When Lucifer was falling from heaven, several other fallen angels, one-third of them, were swept out of the sky with Lucifer's tail and flung to earth.

> Another sign was seen in heaven. Behold, a great red dragon, having seven heads and ten horns, and on his heads seven crowns. His tail drew one third of the stars of the sky and threw them to the earth. (Revelation 12:3–4 WEB)

Fallen angels are also known as demons. They help influence people into doing wrong things. They can possess a body and afflict it with seizures or act in a self-destructive manner. These tempters lure people into believing that their obsessions with sin are okay, "promising them liberty, while they themselves are bondservants of corruption; for a man is brought into bondage by whoever overcomes him" (2 Peter 2:19 WEB). Human desires and passions are not naturally evil, but humans are, however, responsible for controlling them.

"If you do well, won't it be lifted up? If you don't do well, sin crouches at the door. Its desire is for you, but you are to rule over it." (Genesis 4:7 WEB)

Angels who didn't keep their first domain, but deserted their own dwelling place, he has kept in everlasting bonds under darkness for the judgment of the great day. (Jude 1:6 WEB)

But Michael, the archangel, when contending with the devil and arguing about the body of Moses, dared not bring against him an abusive condemnation, but said, "May the Lord rebuke you!" (Jude 1:9 WEB)

For if God didn't spare angels when they sinned, but cast them down to Tartarus, and committed them to pits of darkness to be reserved for judgment. (2 Peter 2:4 WEB)

He said to them, "I saw Satan having fallen like lightning from heaven." (Luke 10:18 WEB)

Then he will say also to those on the left hand, 'Depart from me, you cursed, into the eternal fire which is prepared for the devil and his angels.' (Matthew 25:41 WEB)

Don't you know that we will judge angels? How much more, things that pertain to this life? (1 Corinthians 6:3 WEB)

No temptation has taken you except what is common to man. God is faithful, who will not allow you to be tempted above what you are able but will with the temptation also make the way of escape, that you may be able to endure it. (1 Corinthians 10:13 WEB)

ARCHANGEL LUCIFER

Lucifer in Hebrew means "light bearer." *Satan* in Hebrew means "the adversary." In Greek, *devil* means "false accuser." In the beginning, Lucifer was the most beautiful of all the angels and shined brightest in heaven. Lucifer became very jealous and wanted God's supreme power, so he decided to rebel against God. Satan gathered up and lured other angels to follow him, so God casted them all down from heaven to Earth. This is when the war began: the lifelong spiritual warfare between God, Lucifer, and the fallen angels. Lucifer is depicted with a pitchfork and horns. His color is black. Lucifer is cunning, resourceful, persistent, selfish, very intelligent, and is the master deception. He is the prevaricator, the enemy, the leviathan, the prince of darkness, and prince of the power of the air.

Here is the scripture that describes Lucifer as the most beautiful of all angels:

> "The Lord Yahweh says: 'You were the seal of full measure, full of wisdom, and perfect in beauty. You were in Eden, the garden of God. Every precious stone adorned you: ruby, topaz, emerald, chrysolite, onyx, jasper, sapphire, turquoise, and beryl. Gold work of tambourines and of pipes was in you. They were prepared in the day that you were created. You were the anointed cherub who covers. Then I set you up on the holy

mountain of God. You have walked up and down in the middle of the stones of fire. You were perfect in your ways from the day that you were created, until unrighteousness was found in you. By the abundance of your commerce, your insides were filled with violence, and you have sinned. Therefore, I have cast you as profane out of God's mountain. I have destroyed you, covering cherub, from the middle of the stones of fire. Your heart was lifted up because of your beauty. You have corrupted your wisdom by reason of your splendor. I have cast you to the ground. I have laid you before kings, that they may see you. By the multitude of your iniquities, in the unrighteousness of your commerce, you have profaned your sanctuaries. Therefore, I have brought out a fire from the middle of you. It has devoured you. I have turned you to ashes on the earth in the sight of all those who see you. All those who know you among the peoples will be astonished at you. You have become a terror, and you will exist no more.'" (Ezekiel 28:11–19 WEB)

How art thou fallen from heaven, O Lucifer, son of the morning! how art thou cut down to the ground, which didst weaken the nations! (Isaiah 14:12 KJV)

He said to them, "I saw Satan having fallen like lightning from heaven." (Luke 10:18 WEB)

Another sign was seen in heaven. Behold, a great red dragon, having seven heads and ten horns, and on his heads seven crowns. (Revelation 12:3 WEB)

There was war in the sky. Michael and his angels made war on the dragon. The dragon and his angels made war. They didn't prevail. No place was found for them any more in heaven. The great dragon was thrown down, the old serpent, he who is called the devil and Satan, the deceiver of the whole world. He was thrown down to the earth, and his angels were thrown down with him. (Revelation 12:7–9 WEB)

Be sober and self-controlled. Be watchful. Your adversary, the devil, walks around like a roaring lion, seeking whom he may devour. (1 Peter 5:8 WEB)

and they may recover themselves out of the devil's snare, having been taken captive by him to his will. (2 Timothy 2:26 WEB)

From the time that God created man, Lucifer and the demons that he rules have attacked the Israelites and Christians and wreaked havoc and destruction to our world. Through Jesus Christ, Christians receive a coat of arms to protect them from evil. Apostle Paul describes this as the shield of faith:

Finally, be strong in the Lord, and in the strength of his might. Put on the whole armor of God, that you may be able to stand against the wiles of the devil. For our wrestling is not against flesh and blood, but against the principalities, against the powers, against the world's rulers of the darkness of this age, and against the spiritual forces of wickedness in the heavenly places. Therefore put on the whole armor of God, that you may be able to withstand in the evil day, and having done all, to stand. Stand therefore, having the utility belt of truth buckled around your waist, and having put on the breastplate of righteousness, and having fitted your feet with the preparation of the Good News of peace, above all, taking up the shield of faith, with which you will be able to quench all the fiery darts of the evil one. And take the helmet of salvation, and the sword of the Spirit, which is the word of God; with all prayer and requests, praying at all times in the Spirit, and being watchful to this end in all perseverance and requests for all the saints: on my behalf, that utterance may be given to me in opening my mouth, to make known with boldness the mystery of the Good News, for which I am an ambassador in chains; that in it I may speak boldly, as I ought to speak. (Ephesians 6:10–20 WEB)

So stand tall in your full armor of God and stand firm in your faith in Jesus Christ. Know that the Lord God is always with you, guiding and protecting you through life.

And no wonder, for even Satan masquerades as an angel of light. It is no great thing therefore if his servants also masquerade as servants of righteousness, whose end will be according to their works. (2 Corinthians 11:14–15 WEB)

The Bible has countless stories of battles being fought between the forces of good and the powers of evil. It is called spiritual warfare. The showdown is always between good and evil, right and wrong, truth and light versus deception and darkness. Lucifer really believes he will win this war and take God's most-prized possessions: our souls and ruling this planet. The fall of Lucifer all started when God threw him out of heaven and covered him in maggots because he wanted to proclaim God's throne. Lucifer has been holding a grudge on God for a long, long time because God loves us more than him.

> Your pomp is brought down to Sheol, with
> the sound of your stringed instruments. Maggots
> are spread out under you, and worms cover you.
> (Isaiah 14:11 WEB)

WEAPONS OF A LYING LION

Satan is a lying lion—all mouth full of lies, deception, and false teaching.

> Be sober, be vigilant; because your adversary the devil, as a roaring lion, walketh about, seeking whom he may devour. (1 Peter 5:8 KJV)

> Submit yourselves therefore to God. Resist the devil, and he will flee from you. (James 4:7 KJV)

> Lest Satan should get an advantage of us: for we are not ignorant of his devices. (2 Corinthians 2:11 KJV)

As Christians, we must learn to keep our thoughts pure and good. Have insight to make moral judgments, discerning what is right for God and for you. Pray daily for the helmet of faith to protect your thoughts from the evil one's lies, lies, lies. For if you don't learn to recognize Satan's schemes, his lies will take root in your heart and create a negative emotional reaction like sadness, depression, despair, and hopelessness. These self-critical thoughts are the cause of anxiety, anger, guilt, shame, and embarrassment.

Satan cannot snatch a true believer of Christ from God's hands because Christians are sealed with the Holy Spirit, but his attacks are nonetheless real and can turn a good person into a puddle of mud, seriously oppressing them with his lies and deceptions.

> And I give unto them eternal life; and they shall never perish, neither shall any man pluck them out of my hand. (John 10:28 KJV)

> What? know ye not that your body is the temple of the Holy Ghost, which is in you, which ye have of God, and ye are not your own? (1 Corinthians 6:19 KJV)

> Ye are of God, little children, and have overcome them [demons]: because greater is he [Christ] that is in you, than he [Satan] that is in the world." (1 John 4:4 KJV)

The enemy stands ready to seize people who are engaging in his lies, the ones who are blind and feeling hopelessness. Here is an example of a person standing but has thoughts of worthlessness, then humps over in shame and eventually not being able to walk at all. Finally, they can't feed, clothe, or even speak for themselves, a total negative reaction because of Satan's lies. All because of the lying lion's lies, that person turned into a puddle of mud.

> And that they may recover themselves out of the snare of the devil, who are taken captive by him at his will. (2 Timothy 2:26 KJV)

> Don't you be afraid, for I am with you. Don't be dismayed, for I am your God. I will strengthen you. Yes, I will help you. Yes, I will uphold you with the right hand of my righteousness. (Isaiah 41:10 WEB)

Amen.

As good Christians, be sure that you are listening to words of truth, and be confident that you are speaking in truth to others. Avoid gossip and saying bad things about others. Believe in Christ, and He will transform your life. Build a strong foundation with Jesus, keep your shields of faith on—your helmet will protect you from Satan's lies—hold up your sword, and don't be afraid of the weapons of a lying lion.

THE CHIEF CORNERSTONE

Jesus said to them, "Did you never read in the Scriptures, 'The stone which the builders rejected was made the head of the corner. This was from the Lord. It is marvelous in our eyes'?

"Therefore, I tell you, God's Kingdom will be taken away from you and will be given to a nation producing its fruit. He who falls on this stone will be broken to pieces, but on whomever it will fall, it will scatter him as dust." (Matthew 21:42–44 WEB)

Jesus was referring to the psalms of King David. Now when King David was writing about the chief cornerstone, he was referring to the building of the temple for God.

The stone which the builders rejected has become the cornerstone. This is Yahweh's doing. It is marvelous in our eyes. This is the day that Yahweh has made. We will rejoice and be glad in it! (Psalm 118:22–24 WEB)

The prophet Daniel prophesied to King Nebuchadnezzar about the dream he has of a large statue. It was that all the nations will be crushed by God, and Jesus will be the uncut stone that strikes them down.

> As for this image, its head was of fine gold, its breast and its arms of silver, its belly and its thighs of bronze, its legs of iron, its feet part of iron, and part of clay. You saw until a stone was cut out without hands, which struck the image on its feet that were of iron and clay and broke them in pieces. Then the iron, the clay, the bronze, the silver, and the gold were broken in pieces together, and became like the chaff of the summer threshing floors. The wind carried them away, so that no place was found for them. The stone that struck the image became a great mountain and filled the whole earth. (Daniel 2:32–35 WEB)

> "In the days of those kings the God of heaven will set up a kingdom which will never be destroyed, nor will its sovereignty be left to another people; but it will break in pieces and consume all these kingdoms, and it will stand forever.
> Because you saw that a stone was cut out of the mountain without hands, and that it broke in pieces the iron, the bronze, the clay, the silver, and the gold; the great God has made known to the king what will happen hereafter. The dream is certain, and its interpretation sure." (Daniel 2:44–45 WEB)

The kingdom that God sets up in heaven that will never be destroyed is Jesus's kingdom that will live forever and fill the whole Earth. Daniel prophesied that a man clothed in white will be the son of God.

"I saw in the night visions, and behold, there came with the clouds of the sky one like a son of man, and he came even to the ancient of days, and they brought him near before him. Dominion was given him, and glory, and a kingdom, that all the peoples, nations, and languages should serve him. His dominion is an everlasting dominion, which will not pass away, and his kingdom one that which will not be destroyed." (Daniel 7:13–14 WEB)

All this referencing to the chief cornerstone goes way back to First Kings when King Solomon builds Solomon's Temple.

Behold, I intend to build a house for the name of Yahweh my God, as Yahweh spoke to David my father, saying, 'Your son, whom I will set on your throne in your place shall build the house for my name.' (1 Kings 5:5 WEB)

The house, when it was under construction, was built of stone prepared at the quarry; and no hammer or ax or any tool of iron was heard in the house while it was under construction. (1 Kings 6:7 WEB)

When Solomon's temple was being built, it was forbidden to make any noise near the temple to interrupt worship. So all the chiseling and hammering of these twenty-ton stones had to be done several miles away outside the walls of the city. The Hebrews told of the stories of the construction that was very carefully planned out. Each stone was cut to fit exactly with each other stone. The first stone to be delivered was called the "cornerstone." It was to hold the strength of the entire structure. But when it was delivered, it did not fit, and the workers put it aside to send with the rubbish.

When it came for the capstone to finish with the foundation, no stone fit. So the builder looked for the cornerstone that they had rejected and placed it as the capstone, and it fit perfectly. A head or chief cornerstone is placed above two walls to maintain them together and avoid the building from falling apart. Then all the people and King Solomon recognized what God had done. The builders repented and humbled themselves before the Lord for rejecting the first cut stone.

The stone which the builders refused is become the head stone of the corner. This is the Lord's doing; it is marvelous in our eyes. This is the day which the Lord hath made; we will rejoice and be glad in it. (Psalm 118:22–24 KJV)

Therefore the Lord Yahweh says, "Behold, I lay in Zion for a foundation a stone, a tried stone, a precious cornerstone of a sure foundation. He who believes shall not act hastily." (Isaiah 28:16 WEB)

Then Peter, filled with the Holy Spirit, said to them, "Rulers of the people and elders of Israel: If we this day are judged for a good deed *done* to a helpless man, by what means he has been made well, let it be known to you all, and to all the people of Israel, that by the name of Jesus Christ of Nazareth, whom you crucified, whom God raised from the dead, by Him this man stands here before you whole. This is the 'stone which was rejected by you builders, which has become the chief cornerstone.' Nor is there salvation in any other, for there is no other name under heaven given among men by which we must be saved." (Acts 4:8–12 NKJV)

The chief cornerstone, the rock of salvation, the kingdom of Jesus Christ will fill the whole Earth and the inheritance of our salvation will come to those who believe.

> You also, as living stones, are built up as a spiritual house, to be a holy priesthood, to offer up spiritual sacrifices, acceptable to God through Jesus Christ. Because it is contained in Scripture, "Behold, I lay in Zion a chief cornerstone, chosen and precious: He who believes in him will not be disappointed." (1 Peter 2:5–6 WEB)

> So then you are no longer strangers and foreigners, but you are fellow citizens with the saints and of the household of God, being built on the foundation of the apostles and prophets, Christ Jesus himself being the chief cornerstone; in whom the whole building, fitted together, grows into a holy temple in the Lord; in whom you also are built together for a habitation of God in the Spirit. (Ephesians 2:19–22 WEB)

> He alone is my rock, my salvation, and my fortress. I will never be greatly shaken. (Psalm 62:2 WEB)

I pray that this epic journey with Jesus has illuminated the pages of Scripture and given you peace and joy. May the Lord your God, Jesus Christ, be your chief cornerstone to which you build a strong foundation in His name, sustaining you until He returns. May you live with Jesus in heaven, forever and ever. Amen

ABOUT THE AUTHOR

Karen Marie Parker is an author that delves deeply into the word of God. After a radical conversion in 2014, God took her out of darkness and into the light of Christ. Holy Spirit driven, she has devoted herself to countless Bible studies, the dead sea scrolls' translations, and daily readings from well-known authors, teachers, professors, archaeologists, scholars, theologians, saints, mystics, and pastors like Beth Moore, Thomas Merton, James Finley, Josephus, Sonja Corbitt, Jeff Cavins, Professor Jodi Magness, Professor Jean-Pierre Isbouts, Saint Aquinas, Saint Ignatius, David Limbaugh, Richard Rohr, Max Lucado, and Bishop Robert Barron. Parker's passion for the Word of God has mastered a technique in writing for the layperson to understand sacred Scripture.

Parker is the author of *An Epic Journey through the Holy Bible with Jesus: Volume 1, Volume 2,* and *Volume 3.* She belongs to two Bible study groups and an apostolic Catholic group. She is a member of the St. Matthew's Catholic Church; served two years as a religious education teacher; works through the annual Cum Christo movement; and is mentored by her spiritual director, Sister Regina, from the Emmaus House.

Karen lives in Sidney, Montana, with her husband, Patrick, and their two dogs, Dudar—an English Mastiff—and Delilah—a St. Bernard—along with their precious children and grandchildren.